High School Music Teacher's Handbook

High School Music Teacher's Handbook

A Complete Guide to Managing and Teaching the Total Music Program

Guy S. Kinney

Parker Publishing Company, Inc.
West Nyack, N.Y.

PARKER PUBLISHING COMPANY, INC.
West Nyack, N.Y.

Library of Congress Cataloging-in-Publication Data

Kinney, Guy S.
High school music teacher's handbook.

Bibliography: p.
Includes index.
1. School music--Instruction and study.
2. School music supervision. I. Title.
MT10.K48 1987 780'.7 86-22506

ISBN 0-13-387689-6

Printed in the United States of America

About the Author

Guy S. Kinney is currently a member of the faculty of the North Spencer Christian Academy, Spencer, New York. He was formerly a professional French Hornist with various orchestras, including Principal Hornist with the Birmingham Symphony of Alabama, the Lake George Opera Festival of New York, and a member of the Syracuse Symphony. He is currently Principal Hornist with the Elmira Symphony and the Corning Philharmonic Orchestras of New York. He is also a Hornist with Music International, a performing tour group in Europe.

Mr. Kinney also wrote *Complete Guide to Teaching Small Instrumental Groups in the High School* (Parker Publishing Company, 1980), as well as numerous articles on the subjects of music and religion. Mr. Kinney holds a Bachelor's and Master's Degree in Music and Education, as well as a Master's Degree in Theology.

About This Book

High School Music Teacher's Handbook contains practical, easy-to-use materials for you to use every day in the high school music program. The forms and samples will help you solve such problems as scheduling difficulties, large class size, administrative confusion, inadequate financial resources, heterogeneous grouping of ability and experience levels of your students, and the numerous other details you must cope with in the regular school situation.

This book is packed with suggestions and activities for building a successful music program and for motivating your students. Some examples of these activities can be found in these chapters.

Chapter 1 starts you off by helping you to justify the music program to your administrators. You are given ways for writing your goals and objectives, and communicating these results to others.

Chapter 2 shows you how to achieve personalized instruction and evaluation within the classroom. Included are descriptions of and suggestions for teaching students of various learning rates, and procedures for assessing these students.

Chapter 3 explains how to schedule classes and rehearsals efficiently. You are also given suggestions for working effectively with other staff members and departments in setting up these schedules.

Chapter 4 covers the problems that might arise when putting together concert programs. Solutions to these problems are provided that will make your audience appreciate and respond to your concerts.

Chapter 5 offers tips for presenting assemblies and concerts outside the school. Most community groups appreciate entertainment, so these performances would be a good way for successfully establishing public relations.

Chapter 6 helps you to initiate special projects and music activities that can be done in addition to the regular music class. These include small ensembles that can practice at home, student "coaches," and an after-school instrument repair class.

Chapter 7 offers various techniques for building and maintaining student interest in the music program, such as conducting unusual classes and using team teaching. These will help you motivate your students so they will fully participate in the music program.

Chapter 8 shows how music electives can effectively and efficiently be used in your particular situation to enrich your music program. You are given the answers to such questions as, "How do I actually prepare and teach these electives?" "How do I find materials on the high school level?" and "Can I do the necessary preparation within my already full schedule?"

Chapter 9 introduces you to four creative music classes that you can offer your students. These are contemporary music, electronic music, environmental music, and improvisational music. The necessary equipment and resources needed for each area are listed for you.

Chapter 10 offers suggestions for keeping a simple record system that will free you for important teaching time. Sample forms are given to help you establish your record-keeping system.

Chapter 11 covers fund raising, one of your major concerns because every music department needs money! If you have had unsuccessful experiences in fund-raising ventures, read this chapter for helpful hints and suggestions to make your fund-raising project both successful *and* enjoyable for everyone involved.

Chapter 12 answers your budget and fund-raising questions, such as "What do I do with the money once I have it?" Discussed are such areas as budgeting for sheet music for the chorus, band, or orchestra, budgeting for equipment, and calculating equipment depreciation.

Chapter 13 is a special feature of the *Handbook*, offering detailed teaching tips for wind instruments. Included in this chapter are lists of method books and solo literature to use with both beginning and advanced students.

A complete bibliography of books and articles concludes the book. You can use these as resources for further study.

In short, *High School Music Teacher's Handbook* gives you all the information you need to conduct your high school music program. I hope you'll enjoy using these procedures to make your programs more successful and your students vitally interested in and excited about music.

Guy S. Kinney

Contents

Chapter 1

How to Justify Your Program to the Administration

Music educators have normally spent large parts of their lives involved with music. They have studied it extensively, been involved with it as an avocation, career, or hobby, performed informally, professionally or both, and have developed some type of personal and emotional response to music, whether "on duty" or just at home relaxing. The intrinsic worth of music is something that is rarely thought about. Instead, it is felt inside. It needs no explanation.

As a result, music educators often become defensive, resort to less than objective reasons when asked, and sometimes have difficulty trying to justify our program to the administration or boards of education. We need to clarify our thinking, evaluate our program objectively, and elucidate accomplished goals to demonstrate to those who need to know that our departments are important.

THE IMPORTANCE OF GOALS AND OBJECTIVES

This is an age where cost effectiveness and business management concepts have entered the public schools. In the recent past, many schools were criticized for the lack of operational business acumen. The criticism was not often severe, for money seemed to be easier to come by and prices were much lower. Communities did not seem to mind the tax revenues needed to support local school programs. After all, school populations were expected to continue to grow. New schools, expanded staffs, and additional equipment were needed to maintain this upward thrust.

Suddenly, we have entered an era of skyrocketing prices, reduced student populations, and unbelievable energy costs. Communities are paying more for smaller staffs, less equipment, and lower student enrollment. In the taxpayers' eyes, something is wrong. They have good reasons to question school authorities.

The administration, on the other hand, is faced with a shrinking dollar, higher salary demands, and accountability to the taxpayers and their representatives, the Board of Education. School superintendents and principals must be surer now than at any other time about the soundness of their programs. They must carefully weigh costs in every department, cut where they can, maintain only that which can prove its value to the school, and still meet state-mandated requirements.

Within the school are the individual departments, such as the music department. Each thinks its reason for being there is self-explanatory. But with cost effectiveness considered, every department must be able to justify itself, prove its worth, and give an account of itself to the administration.

Departments that prove valuable in the eyes of the administration, the community, and the students will be left basically untouched. They will be funded and scheduled. Weaker departments will be trimmed, reduced, and possibly even eliminated as a school-supported function.

These thoughts are not presented as scare tactics, nor are they an attempt to paint a bleak picture of the future in education. Rather, they are written, and should be viewed, as regular occurrences in school districts throughout the land. We, as music educators, must not be complacent about our departments. We must not assume that there will always be band, chorus, or orchestra. We must not be defensive about our curriculum. Instead, we should take the initiative. We should show, by results that can be explained to the nonmusician, why our program is important and why school support should continue. We need to go one step further than mere accountability. We should be so strong and important in the eyes of the community and administration that *they* will defend us, *they* will demand financial support, and *they* will not even consider us at budget-cutting time.

ASSESSING YOUR ACHIEVEMENTS OBJECTIVELY

When the intrinsic value of music study is considered, the sense of worth felt in its pursuit and the results seen in students' attitudes, our emotional response is often difficult to put into words. Thus, when attempting to assess the achievements of the music department, it is not often done so objectively. Music educators often write with their feelings rather than their intellects, but as the aforementioned discussion points out, they must build their accountability on an objective basis. Nonmusicians will be able to relate to an objective analysis, not to a subjective musical discussion of the results. Two things should be done carefully:

1. writing objectives
2. evaluating results

Writing objectives is both efficient and simple. Nevertheless, there are many misunderstandings that should be clarified in order to establish curricular objective data carefully and accurately. Also, it is important that you assess the results accurately.

WRITING OBJECTIVES AND EVALUATING THE RESULTS

When writing objectives, the end results of the plan are the important considerations. For instance, when the lesson, class, program, or school year is over, what is the final behavior you expect the students to acquire? Results must be measured in objective terms. Or, more succinctly, what is the "terminal behavior"? As Robert Mager puts it:

> Since no one can see into another's mind to determine what he knows, you can only determine the state of the learner's intellect or skill by observing some aspects of his behavior or performance (the term "behavior," as used here, means overt action).[1]

Identifying this overt action, either verbal or nonverbal, means that you can evaluate the results of the objectives. For instance, the terminal behavior might state that the "student can play scales in all flat keys, on quarter note rhythms, in a moderate tempo (96-108 beats per minute)."

Another consideration in writing objectives includes using words that mean what you say and will mean the same thing to someone else. Mager again points out some aspects that can be open to misinterpretation and are hard to define:

to know
to really understand
to grasp the significance of
to believe[2]

However, other words are less apt to be misinterpreted. These might include:

to recite
to identify
to solve
to contrast[3]

Another important aspect of writing objectives is the establishment of the degree of technical mastery of a plan. In other words, to *what extent* is the learner expected to be able to do something? For instance, in an instrumental music lesson, you may state that the object is to learn scales. Yet a further clarification will be to establish what scales, how many, how fast, and in what rhythmic patterns the students will be expected to master them.

It is important that these specific steps be taken so that the administration, which may not be musically inclined, can relate to and understand them. Therefore, the three basic steps in writing objectives will include:

1. identifying terminal behavior
2. the resultant learning
3. degree of mastery expected in specific language

Remember that objectives are merely your intents regarding a course or class lesson. Your results may not be positive. If so, this can be a real learning experience for you! You will be able to evaluate your technique in teaching and the methods used to achieve it.

EFFECTIVELY COMMUNICATING THE RESULTS TO THE ADMINISTRATION

There are various ways and methods to communicate effective results of music study to the administration. Indeed, it is extremely important that this be done as carefully and as regularly as possible. In fact, there may be times when you will be able to present your results to the Board of Education. Any time you communicate with the administration, or you are asked to give a report, there are some essential considerations. Among these will be the method of reporting. To be specific, reports are either oral or written.

Giving Oral Reports

Should you be asked to present your department's objectives, goals, evaluations, or any other aspect, you should carefully prepare what you are going to say in advance. A long, rambling, disjointed talk will not only be unproductive and a waste of time, but it will probably bore the board members. One way to avoid this is to write out your talk on small (3 × 5 inch) index cards in *outline* form. Only the specific facts will be listed. Only the important points will be noted. Make sure the outline includes an introduction (plans, projects, purposes); then follow this by the methods (actual steps taken to achieve the above) to be used. The conclusion will include the results of all the steps in the outline. Remember to keep your oral report short and specific, and *do not* deviate from the outline.

Sample Outline for Oral Report

I. Introduction: To Establish a Comprehensive High School Music Major Program
 A. Major concerns
  1. finance
  2. scheduling
  3. motivating the students to participate
II. Implementing the Program
 A. Rescheduling existing faculty
 B. Sticking within overall music budget
 C. Needs (if any) of additional funding
  1. reasons for needs
  2. alternatives (if funds are not available)
III. Course Requirements
 A. Core requirements
  1. band
  2. chorus
  3. orchestra
  4. music theory
  5. music history
 B. Electives (two required)
  1. American music
  2. folk music
  3. electronic music

IV. Program results
    A. Number of students participating
        1. vocal
        2. instrumental
    B. Number of music major students
    C. Student survey results
    D. Teachers' feelings on the programs

Finally, it is important that you anticipate questions by Board members. There will usually be members on the Board who are not that familiar with your department or even its full scope. Try to think ahead of time about the probable questions that will be asked. If you do this, you will not be so apt to be caught off guard by questions you cannot answer quickly. Nevertheless, there may be questions you cannot readily answer. Should this occur, do not be afraid to say that you do not know but will try to find the answer. This is a much better policy than trying to invent an answer on the spot.

Writing Reports As Memos

At times your school administration will request that you give a written report instead of an oral one. The same procedures should be used as those in an oral presentation. Write in a succinct manner, use an outline (but use the outline titles as subheadings to the various sections in the report). Do not get carried away with your literary style or colorful prose. Stick to the basics. Board members have a lot to do and are not usually interested in reading reams of paper.

Write your report as a memo (see Figure 1-1). In this way it will be immediately clear what the report is about and to whom it is addressed. This is important when considering the many reports the Board reads and their need to establish priorities in their agenda.

UNDERSTANDING WHAT THE ADMINISTRATION EXPECTS OF YOU

Recently the term "accountability" has been heard during faculty meetings and written in administrative memos. The accountability factor in teacher's contracts is expected to be implemented in the

TO: Board of Education
FROM: Guy Kinney
RE: Development of comprehensive music curriculum
DATE: June 14, 19xx

Major Concerns in the Program

Implementing the Program

Course Requirements

Program Results

Figure 1-1

near future throughout the country. However, there are certain questions that must be asked by the teacher as well as the administration.

Joseph Labuta states the answer to the question "To what extent are teachers liable?" authoritatively. "A teacher should not be held accountable unless he knows at the outset the educational results for which he is responsible."[4] In other words, administrations or boards of education should not use the word accountability to their employees without first giving them direction as to their expectations. A professional performing musician receives compensation from an employer by playing some particular music. Both the musician and the employer understood before the concert what is expected and what compensation is to be given.

If teachers are given clear directions as to what their responsibilities are, then perhaps the resultant evaluations by the administration will be sufficient to establish an accountability factor. Furthermore, those teachers who greatly exceed the areas for which they are responsible can be evaluated fairly and perhaps compensated by merit increases or some other form of employment benefits.

HOW TO CHANGE FOR THE BETTER

To implement good behavioral objectives successfully as part of an accountability agreement between the teacher and the administration, an assessment must be made. This may be accomplished by the teacher and administration's interpreting the terminal behavior and measuring the resultant learning through standardized tests. In the case of music, you might request that a performance of the expected materials be presented and graded.

Because assessment "indicates the degree of instructional effectiveness,"[5] it is important that it be done carefully and accurately. Assessment "determines if the designated behaviors have in fact been acquired.[6] In addition, it can be of great benefit to the teacher in demonstrating clearly to the administration the effectiveness of the instructional program.

However, before the administration evaluates the program, you can check to see if the instructional objectives are being met and are progressing regularly throughout the school year. In this manner, it will be possible to check for deficiencies in either the students' responses (correct musical learning or performing) or your own instruction. If you find that your method of teaching is not working well, you can then alter and improve it. Notwithstanding the fact that it is humbling to find your methods wanting, you can take comfort in knowing that no less a genius than Beethoven himself constantly revised and reworked his music until it was *just right!* In fact, if we look at his notebooks, the earliest renditions of some of his most famous works look very poor in comparison to his final and, seemingly, *almost perfect* products. It is *no disgrace* to improve oneself.

Should your first suggestion of less-than-acceptable performance come from the administration before they begin evaluations, do not take offense. We all have things that could be improved. It is important to remember that administrations do not evaluate programs in order to find fault but to assess the relative value and performance standards of their schools. Therefore, do not be hurt, ashamed, or indignant if it is pointed out to you that various things should and could be done to improve your teaching or the department.

Isolating Weak Areas and Strengthening Positive Ones

Sometimes it is difficult to understand just where the weak areas are. Trying to isolate each aspect of the instructional program and the concomitant behavioral objectives will allow you to measure all areas of the curriculum. This can be done simply by examining each objective (goal) that is written down at the beginning of the instruction period. You can analyze data as shown in Figure 1-2. An example of a completed plan is provided in Figure 1-3.

In Figure 1-3, you can easily isolate and understand the results of the objective because it is detailed and easily interpreted. By incorporating all of your objectives, you have an accurate assessment of each separate unit and should be able to ascertain the needs to improve weak areas. In addition, you can immediately recognize those strong aspects of your objectives. Thus, you will have an approach to your program that will enable you to correct the inefficient sections and reinforce the successful ones.

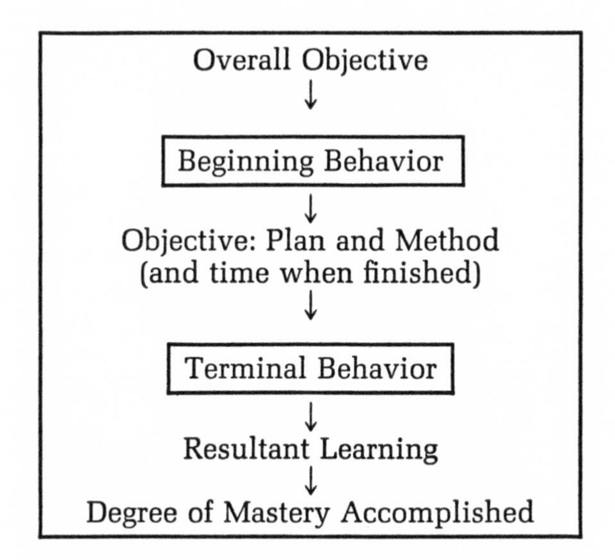

Figure 1-2

Objective: To Understand and Identify Baroque Styles of Music

I. Beginning Behavior — Students know only general concepts of serious music, pop, or folk. No studies in specific periods have been taken.

A. Objectives:
1. Students will identify Baroque composers including Bach, Handel, Purcell, Vivaldi, Corelli.
2. Students will identify, by listening, Baroque music as opposed to Classical or Romantic styles.
3. Students will be given written and oral tests to measure results.

B. Method: lecture, records, live in-class performances

C. Time: four weeks

II. Terminal Behavior

A. Resultant Learning:
1. Students can identify, by sight and listening, Baroque styles, as opposed to other periods of music, and receive 90 percent or better accuracy.
2. Students can identify, by written tests, Baroque qualities and composers.

B. Degree of Mastery Accomplished:
1. Students are familiar with Baroque forms: fugue, oratorio, concerto grosso, cantata, and recitative-aria vocal selections.
2. Students know lives of Handel, Bach, Vivaldi, Corelli, and Purcell.
3. Students can identify, by listening, and are familiar especially with:
   a. "Trumpet Voluntary," Purcell (Clark)
   b. "Messiah," Handel
      (1) Arias
      (2) Chorus
   c. "Violin Concerto in A Minor," Vivaldi
   d. "Suite for Strings," Corelli
   e. "Prelude and Fugue in G Minor," Bach
   f. "Concerto (Brandenburg 2) Grosso," Bach

Figure 1-3

Having a Good Public Relations Program

A statement about the importance of maintaining a positive image in your overall music department comes from Mr. Labuta again:

> Although no one can deny that musical performance is essential to the music program, group performance alone is no longer accepted as a measure of musical accountability. Accountability means that music teachers are responsible for the learning of each individual pupil as well as for the training of bands, orchestras and choruses.[7]

Perhaps in the future, not only will concerts and marching events not be held in overall esteem, but the individual learning of each student will be measured and considered by administrators. As a result, we should be ready to utilize all our objectives in teaching, to report them accurately, to incorporate performances as *part* (not all) of a well-rounded music program and to be sure that our public relations program includes all aspects of the music activities. In so doing you will have a situation where those who know can defend your program, along with yourself, articulately and convincingly.

A strong public relations program is a tremendous asset to any program, especially to a music department. Not only will you gain the support of parents and students, but the administration will include these supporting groups in their evaluation of the department's accountability.

> A good public relations program is imperative for a music department. The best protection that can be given is a solid base of support from both the administration and the community. Pressure exerted by the community upon the Board of Education can be a major factor in the retention of a well-run music program. School boards are reluctant to cut popular programs that can lead to community resentment and backfire when it comes to vote on proposed annual budgets.[8]

A few basic steps will help you establish a good public relations program that will reach the maximum number of people. Included in these steps are the different categories of the music department's responsibilities—teaching, performing, inspiring. Summarized briefly, in Figure 1-4, are the categories and techniques for beginning your program.

Using Figure 1-4, you can check on your program and its effectiveness. You can also decide if some of the points are missing from your program. If used correctly, public relations tools will help you establish good accountability in your school situation.

Teaching

Media Attention

A. Posters in conspicuous corridor places
   1. highlights of courses taught
   2. student projects
   3. photographs of musicians relative to courses
B. Announcements over the public address system regarding the class's activities[9]
   1. special student projects
   2. trips
   3. performances

Performing

A. News release of concerts
   1. radio, newspapers, television
   2. posters
   3. announcements
B. Photos and prizes won
   1. set-up displays in corridors
   2. photos sent to newspapers

Inspiring

A. Inspirational activities reaching the largest number of people
   1. parades
   2. civic functions
   3. clubs and community groups
   4. school concerts and assemblies
B. Communication of special programs, and their importance.

Figure 1-4.

CHAPTER 1 ENDNOTES

1. Mager, Robert F. *Preparing Instructional Objectives.* Palo Alto, CA: Fearon Publishers, 1962, 13.

2. *Ibid.*, p.11.

3. *Ibid.*, p.11

4. Labuta, Joseph A. *Guide to Accountability in Music Instruction.* West Nyack, NY: Parker Publishing Co. 1974, 23.

5. *Ibid.*, p. 117.

6. *Ibid.*, p. 117.

7. *Ibid.*, p. 20.

8. Kinney, Guy S. *Complete Guide to Teaching Small Instrumental Groups in the High School.* West Nyack, NY: Parker Publishing Co., 1980, 241.

9. Too often the announcements, other than administrative, are mostly about the sports programs and game results. While this is perfectly all right, the other school departments and activities should avail themselves of opportunities for visibility within the school.

Chapter 2

Ways to Achieve Personalized Instruction and Evaluation in Class

Various school districts organize music classes in a variety of ways. Some have music classes every day; others only once a week. Some courses have large numbers of students; others are small. Two things most music classes have in common, regardless of size, are the problems inherent in teaching students of different abilities and experience, and of trying to achieve some sort of individualized instruction within the large class framework.

Sometimes music teachers tend to give up on that possibility and just go through the lesson, letting the chips of knowledge fall where they may and forgetting about individual attention (except for discipline cases) altogether. But it is not as hopeless as it may seem. There are some solutions that do work, that are effective, and that will result in a better class learning rate.

These solutions may include proven methods for overcoming the problems of different rates of achievement among students. Sometimes they may include special activities for faster students that can be done using other students as guides. Also, motivation of the slower students may be achieved in classroom, instrumental, or vocal teaching situations. Finally, effective strategies for evaluating the results may be used.

HOW TO OVERCOME PROBLEMS OF LEARNING AND ACHIEVEMENT RATES

One of the most frustrating experiences a music teacher faces is what to do about the individual rates at which students in a class learn. Some catch on quickly; others need more time or even an extended study of certain materials before going on. Some students, who are quicker, become bored after being held back to let the slower ones catch up.

Yet it is possible to make the lesson a challenging learning experience for all. If a little preparation on your part is taken, you can be effective with each student in the class. First, it is not unkind or prejudicial to understand one of the basic aspects of learning. Slower students will pick up information and facts and acquire some understanding from the faster ones. Therefore, if the quicker students are motivated and encouraged, they not only will not become bored, but also the slower ones will learn some concepts from them. Conversely, if too much time is spent with the slower students, the brighter ones will not learn effectively and may become dissatisfied or listless with the proceedings.

However, this in no way implies a sort of benign neglect towards the slower students. It *is* our job to try to reach *all* students, both the brighter *and* the less quick ones. And there are some things we can do to help motivate those who take longer in their studies.

Helping the Slower Students

Slower students can be helped in music by simplifying the music slightly. For instance, in vocal or instrumental classes a simplified part will often help the less experienced students sing or play their parts with others. For example, here is a selection that may be too difficult for some students to play:

Should technical considerations be too difficult, you can make the part easier by simplifying the rhythm. For instance, taking out the thirty-second notes and perhaps even the sixteenths will alleviate some of the difficulty.

As the student begins to understand the rhythm and can master the technical proficiency, you can help him progress from the second to the first illustration. Thus, he or she will gradually attain the desired level of technique.

In simplifying the part and by progressively moving the student toward the more difficult sections, keep motivation high. The resultant boredom that slower students often exhibit when they cannot perform a specific selection is often caused by an attitude of frustration that leads to giving up. The simplified technique approach will dissipate the boredom. Students will remain interested and you can see and hear results.

Motivation and How It Can Help Slower Students

The musical examples on page 20 can help slow students learn. There are others that can be used in all aspects of the music program—instrumental, vocal, and classroom. But here it might be good to discuss some aspects of motivation itself. In *Secondary School Music*, the authors describe musical motivation as follows:

> True motivation is self-motivation. In a music class, the highest form of motivation is a desire to learn music. The student who performs well is generally the student who practices without pressure. He establishes his own goals and attains them. He constantly evaluates his own progress. To teachers, this points the way for class activities. Every class is important and needs to be planned to meet the needs of individuals in the group.[1]

The last sentence in the preceding quote is one of the most important for the teacher. Every class *must be planned* to meet the needs of *individuals* in the group. Often, teachers see different periods during the day as pertaining to different "classes"—whole groups of students whom they are trying to teach. Yet these classes contain *individuals* who need to be reached as individuals—not groups. Each student has a unique potential and a purpose in life that teachers should try to help him or her reach. You must always keep this in mind.

Jesse Stuart tells a story about his days as a Kentucky school teacher and about a young boy in his class who was always doing "weird things" and conducting "strange" experiments. Such examples included his jumping up and down in one spot and trying to figure out why he didn't land several miles away each time he jumped because of the earth's rotation. Other students couldn't figure him out, and he didn't concentrate on his prescribed studies all that well. After he left school, several years later he dropped from sight and no one knew where he was. Jesse Stuart assumed he must be in prison. But shortly thereafter he learned that the boy was in a top secret installation in California where he had been a scientist working on the development of the atomic bomb.[2]

Reaching individuals like the one described by Jesse Stuart is what education is all about. It is the guiding, the developing, the structuring of young minds so that they can reach their own individual potentials.

Keeping Slower Students in Large Groups Motivated

In Chorus. One way to help slower students in a large ensemble and keep their interest high is to seat them alternately beside better students. In chorus, this should work fairly easily. A strong singer on either side will help the slower student find the pitch and be "carried along" by the others. It will also encourage the student by keeping him or her from being lost all the time.

In Bands and Orchestras. Trying to seat slower players next to faster ones in bands and orchestras may be more difficult than with a chorus. Some instrumental sections may not be large enough to provide alternate seating. Perhaps the flute, clarinet, and violin sections will be quite large. But the baritone, horn, oboe, viola, saxophone, and other instrumental sections may be too small. Attempt alternate seating, but if it is not possible, there is an alternative. Seat sections that play similar parts next to each other. In bands, this may include tenor saxophones, trombones, and baritones, or alto clarinets, alto saxophones, and horns. In orchestras, the first and second violin sections could be together, and the celli and double basses could be close together.

In such a manner as the above, you can maintain a close proximity between the slower and faster students, and the slower ones will be helped by the faster ones. In addition, you must maintain patience with these players. It is often frustrating to try to make music with some student who cannot play the parts correctly. There is a tendency to take this frustration out on the students. But remember, they are trying! Be patient and give them all the time they need. Often the best thing to do is simply not try so hard with the student. Encourage him or her, but let the student learn at his or her own pace. Don't expect them to master each technique in one lesson, but if these players can be near the faster ones, they will be able to maintain a reference point in the music.

In the Classroom. In junior and senior high music classes, the students are often of mixed abilities. This is usually because music classes are not always mandatory, but rather elective in nature. The students who sign up for these electives will come from various places in the school curriculum. In some classes, such as high school music theory, music history, or musical theater, there not only will be students of various academic levels, but the groups will also contain students of many different musical backgrounds. Some will have had extensive music reading experiences; others will come into the class with little or no formal music training.

Organizing Special Activities for Faster Students

Your problem as a classroom music teacher will be to sustain motivation and help each individual, whether the class is an elective or a required course. The slower students obviously will need more attention than the brighter or more experienced ones. Therefore, a way to approach this is to assign the faster students special projects or research that may be done in another room or in the school library. By arranging the schedule ahead of time you can have those students go to the library and work, leaving you free to spend some much needed time with those who need it. However, try not to assign busy work to the students; instead, assign something that will be a learning process for them. One day a week or every other week may be all you will need. Just a few minutes concentrating with the slower students will do much by way of remediation.

Brighter or quicker students will need to be kept motivated and challenged or they, too, will lose interest. Yet it is surprising how many music teachers simply let the quicker students be held back with the rest of the class, when they could achieve much more. Moving the brighter students to fulfill their potential remains a major challenge to music educators.

Solving Some Unique Instrumental and Choral Problems

Due to a lack of scheduling flexibility, it is often impossible to give the better students private or semiprivate lessons. They are sometimes scheduled in vocal and instrumental classes of a fairly large size. How to let them move ahead while the rest of the group moves at a slower pace is the question. If we simply assign lessons further in the lesson book, these students will achieve more. Yet during their class lesson, they will usually have to go back and play with the rest of the class. This can become boring for them.

One method that has proven successful is to assign graded solos to these students. This becomes extra work, in addition to the regularly assigned lesson material. The students will be able to progress as they master one level of solos and move on to the next higher one. Solos are musically interesting as well as challenging. Students usually have a feeling of pride in doing something as a solo, even if they do not perform it in public. And solos can take the place of etudes, especially if they are picked for certain technical problems that need to be mastered.

When brighter students study solos, they will not become so bored when forced to go more slowly in the lesson books with the class during lesson times. If you are not familiar with the graded lists of solos available, the following is a sample of places to look in trying to find suitable works at various levels of difficulty:

1. The New York State School Music Association's *Official Manual of Graded Music*. Contact: Robert Campbell, Executive Secretary/Treasurer, Editorial Office, 108 Brandywine Avenue, Schenectady, NY 12307.
2. Reviews published and graded in *The Instrumentalist*. Contact: The Instrumentalist Co., 1418 Lake Street, Evanston, IL 60204.
3. Some publishers' own graded recommendations on their works.

How to Help Faster Students in the Classroom

During music electives or required classes that are taught in a classroom situation, there are certain ways to help the quicker students achieve their potentials and keep them interested. Here is a brief suggested list of things to do:

1. Students can be assigned special projects to do in the library, another room, or at home. Such things as composing and/or arranging and orchestrating a work that is being studied can be done. Performing the finished product will add a sense of completeness and an understanding of that which goes into the music business.
2. Students can do individual research that, although not necessarily written up in essay form, could be written on note cards and presented orally to the class. Composers, development of styles or instruments, historical backgrounds, mechanics of musical sound (acoustics), and many other topics could be used on a semiregular basis.
3. Using student guides as an effective way to help some of the slower students can be most helpful. Tutoring is both a

learning experience for the student being helped and for the student doing the tutoring. Eric Leidzen, the noted composer, once said, "When you start to teach, that is when you begin to learn."[3] (Note: Student guides or tutors *do not* take the place of the teacher. Rather, they act in conjunction with the teacher. Uncertified instructors should be used to assist, never to be used in place of a regular teacher.)

HOW TO EVALUATE STUDENTS' PROGRESS

Music, especially the performing aspect of it, is a less objective subject to try to evaluate. As each student studies his or her instrument or voice, each will, in turn, develop at a different rate of progress. To evaluate each student fully, you must be able to identify the individual potentials, innate abilities, efforts, attitudes, and numerous other factors that often become too complicated to isolate effectively. Therefore, there is much subjectivity that goes into a musical evaluation.

For instance, in a music lesson, is the student marked on notes or rhythmic perfection? Does musical interpretation become part of the mark? If so, how is it considered? What is the scale used? Are all students marked the same way in that particular lesson or are individual differences in talent taken into consideration? What about tone quality?

These considerations become items that *must* be taught about before any type of musical evaluation can be attempted. However, if they are considered and a similar scale is used for all students, it is possible to come up with a fairly accurate grade or mark that may be used as a reference point for further guidance.

Using the Personal Evaluation Form

One system of evaluating students that is both beneficial to the student and appreciated by the parents is the "Personal Evaluation Form," which was developed for the purpose of giving a clear picture of how well the student is doing in musical performance study. The form, shown in Figure 2-1, explains to the parents not only the reasons for the form but also the individual characteristics taken into consideration.

Personal Evaluation Form

Dear Parent:

Through past experience, it is felt that most parents are very interested in the progress of their children in educational activities. It is also felt that many parents are not really aware of the success or failure of their children in instrumental music. While a quarterly report is sent home with the student, music, being a less objective (right or wrong) type of subject, requires a more extensive analysis than the numerical grade can ever show.

Therefore, the high school instrumental department is sending an evaluation sheet home for your benefit. The attached sheet attempts to clarify a little better the student's progress, abilities, attitudes, and level of musicality.

This form is only to inform you more fully and perhaps help the student in his or her instrumental/vocal success in school; it is hoped that this report will be helpful to you, too.

Sincerely,

Guy Kinney
Chairman
Music Department

Enc.

Student's Name ______________________

Material and/or Area Evaluated
____
____

Tone ______________
Control ___________
Range ____________
Clearness _________

Attitude:

Technique __________
Fingering __________
Missed Notes _______
Articulation _______

Special Considerations:

Rhythm ______	Teacher Comments:
Tempo ______	
Counting ______	
Steady Beat ______	
Musicality ______	
Interpretation ______	
Overall ______	
Dynamics ______	Future Recommendations:
Forte (full) ______	
Piano (soft) ______	
Flexibility ______	

Recommended to Stay in Group ______

Recommended to Drop in Band ______

Conference with Parent Requested ______

Figure 2-1

Important Points to Remember in Evaluation

The advantages of using the "Personal Evaluation Form" include demonstrating the efforts that the students may have put into the study (Special Considerations) and the general attitude displayed in the class or lesson. Parents may then be able to understand a little better why the student did or did not do as well as expected.

There are certain standards that should be used whenever evaluation procedures are initiated. These standards (or criteria) will have a direct effect upon the validity of the final report. Let's examine some general concepts:

1. The report must be valid in its conclusion. In other words, the evaluation should measure what it claims to measure.
2. Practical results should be the main emphasis. The evaluation should concentrate on how well the student did that which was assigned—not necessarily any form of music that *might* have been used or *should* have been used.

3. Be specific. Evaluate specific aspects as clearly as possible so that those who read it can understand exactly *where* the student is strong or weak.
4. Try to maintain a positive attitude. For example, one person may read an automobile's gas gauge as half empty and another as half full. A student can be said to have failed 50 percent of the work or to have achieved 50 percent of the requirements. The way something is stated can mean a lot in the general attitude of the parents or person who reads the report.

VOCAL PROBLEMS AND HOW TO WORK THEM OUT

Some areas of vocal music programs that seem troublesome and cause frustration on the part of the director include: lack of music reading, inadequate vocal lessons or instruction, lack of outside practice, and students' not taking choral participation seriously as an academic study. Certainly, there are numerous programs in the schools whereby the above considerations are met effectively. There are vocal programs even in the middle school areas where the students achieve levels that will amaze everyone. I once had the privilege of working as a member of a professional orchestra that was hired to accompany a junior high chorus (grades seven through nine) in the complete and uncut presentation of the oratorio "King David" by Honegger. The director, Laurence Pivachek of Oneida Junior High School in Schenectady, New York, regularly did concerts of that caliber with his group. This is one example; there are many others.

It has been my observation, after discussions with many vocal teachers, that the general trend in many junior and senior high choruses is towards "in-school work" only. That is, the only thing that gets done in vocal work is done in the rehearsals. There is very little outside preparation being done on the part of the students. Band directors, on the other hand, take it for granted that their students will at least do some practicing (hoping for a lot!) at home. What are the answers to the vocal teacher's dilemma?

Some remedies can effectively be introduced into the program to motivate the students to achieve a level with their voices (their instruments) that the other music students do in the instrumental classes. Take each area of recognized weakness individually.

Music Reading and How to Teach It

If there is not much time available to teach music reading alone, some of it can and should be done during the regular choral rehearsal. The best time is immediately after the warm-up. Many directors say they can't afford the time because they are pressed for upcoming concerts or festivals. But, in truth, they *cannot afford not to*! A little teaching of music reading at the beginning of rehearsals will pay dividends. In fact, it doesn't have to take a lot of time. Rather, certain basic fundamentals of singing by sight can be taught in just a few minutes at each rehearsal. The simplest to most complicated techniques can be learned easily if used consistently. Below is an example of a simple music reading exercise.

In other words, simple solfege is the best and most solid method of teaching vocal music reading. The tones do, mi, sol will be later used as a reference point to travel on to lesser-known and more difficult sequences, such as this:

By continuing up the ladder of difficulty, the choir will improve its ability to read music individually—slowly at first—but then, later, it will begin to be transferred to various types of music the group may encounter. The important thing, however, is to continue the drilling on a regular rehearsal-by-rehearsal basis. Do not give up. Eventually, the entire chorus *will* learn to read the printed page.

How to Overcome the Lack of Vocal Lessons

Many school vocal programs do not have vocal instruction. Lessons are nonexistent, and it is difficult to teach vocal techniques to the students. While it may not be possible to schedule actual lessons in the music curriculum, there are some alternatives to use in order to teach at least a minimum of instructional methods.

One method of teaching vocal techniques is to schedule vocal sectionals. It students are not allowed to leave classes for this, or if there is no regular period available during the day, you might take a survey to determine how many students are free at any given time. It is often possible to schedule several students for sectional practice during study halls or free time. Usually, this will mean that the group will be mixed—maybe three sopranos, one alto, four tenors, and one bass, or some such group. But remember that your main emphasis will be to *teach* vocal techniques, not necessarily rehearse the choral music being prepared for the next concert.

Should this system be put into practice, those students who couldn't be scheduled at all during the day might be asked to attend a one-day-a-week after-school session. Scheduling such a session is certainly not ideal. Yet it is an effective remedy to *no instruction at all*!

How to Overcome the Lack of Outside Vocal Practice

It is interesting to note that when there is proper motivation, students will practice outside the classroom situation. Where there doesn't seem to be any compelling reason, they will tend not to practice. When I directed a church choir on a regular basis, I was always surprised to discover that whenever we began rehearsals for a special event, such as a choir concert or cantata, the choir members would take it upon themselves to go to each other's homes and learn their parts. However, in the school situation, very little of this is ever done.

Perhaps additional motivation could be instilled by singing all or part of a forthcoming concert at an unusual location. Students often become complacent with the routine of regular in-school concerts. If, just before the scheduled concert, the chorus could present special music at a community group's meeting, it would give two additional benefits. First, pubic relations are enhanced with a school group performing at the local Rotary association or Lodge meeting. Second, students will be motivated to learn their music well through outside preparation in order to do a good job. Most often, community organizations—whether civic, private or religious—will be most congenial and appreciative of your group's providing their evening's entertainment.

The incentive needed is provided by these extra events in which your vocal groups can participate. Students will almost always come through with their preparation when they feel personally needed. It does seem, however, that public school organizations do not always take enough advantage of these ready-made opportunities to perform. One word of caution, however; don't overdo it. Performing too many events may cause the students, once again, to become complacent and the organizations to begin to feel that you should be there. Use these events sparingly, carefully, and with preparation.

How to Instill a Serious Attitude toward Vocal Participation

In many schools, choral organizations rehearse during an activity or "free" period. Thus, students who are scheduled for study halls come down and sign up for chorus. Some may even sign up simply to avoid study hall and to have something to do. The result is that many students do not take their participation very seriously.

A prevailing practice in many schools is allowing any student to participate in music. Instrumental study requires an instrument, instruction, and some outside practice in order to perform with any kind of proficiency. However, vocal students often have the idea that "anyone can sing" and that their voices really aren't their instruments. Thus, they do not feel the need to practice or study.

This view is wrong. A voice is an instrument. It is, perhaps, the most efficient and perfect of all. It needs careful instruction and regular practice.

Some things that can be done to help overcome these attitudes may be in the enrollment procedures. Students could sign up in the following ways:

1. The course is set up for credit. Requirements will mean *acceptable* (to the instructor) preparation and participation. Grades are given on report cards.
2. Individual placement auditions upon entering. Only those students who know the music will be allowed to continue in the group.
3. General acceptance auditions for any students wishing to join; in other words, a select choir.

A FINAL WORD

Trying to achieve some sort of personalized instruction with your students in a large class or performing group setting is often a frustrating and complicated situation. With the suggestions in this chapter, there remains one basic ingredient without which failure still may be looming. That one ingredient is perseverance! Keep trying, persevere, search for that way to reach Billy in the last row or Sharon on the left—do not quit trying. Remember: Those warm bodies in your room are sensitive, important human beings.

CHAPTER 2 ENDNOTES

1. Glenn, Neal E., William B. McBride, and George H. Wilson. *Secondary School Music*. Englewood Cliffs, NJ: Prentice-Hall, 1970, 75.

2. Stuart, Jesse. *To Teach, to Love*. New York: World Publishing Co., 1970.

3. As told to James Burke, solo cornetist.

Chapter 3

How to Simplify Department Scheduling

One of the most important aspects of a well-run music department is efficient scheduling, which can contribute most effectively to the success or failure of the program. Students who have to drop music studies because of other academic conflicts are often your better students. As disastrous as this can be to a department, it does often occur. Therefore, to facilitate scheduling, to avoid conflicts, and to anticipate problems is to understand the major areas of potential problems in your program.

Several areas of help are available, and when conflicts do occur there are alternatives that can be tried in order to fit those students who seemingly have conflicting requirements with their other classes and activities into the music program. In addition, there are several possibilities when scheduling rehearsal times for large performing groups, ensembles, class, and individual lessons.

Scheduling music activities as part of the regular curriculum, as an extracurricular program, in school, or after school will be something the music staff will have to decide. The administration and the guidance department should work with the staff to avoid unnecessary conflicts. Some are unavoidable, but others can be overcome if careful attention is given to scheduling procedures.

STAFFING, SCHEDULING CLASSES, REHEARSALS, AND LESSONS

Scheduling music classes often presents problems that other courses do not face. One problem is the nature of the high school program itself, in that many of the music groups are cross-sectional; that is, grades nine to twelve are included in one rehearsal time. On the other hand, other courses in the school are usually intended for a one-grade level. Therefore, it is more likely that students will be free for these other classes.

Various alternatives are available when trying to schedule music classes, rehearsals, and music group registrations. Examine the representative music department offerings individually.

Scheduling Bands, Choruses, and Orchestras First

Probably the best way to establish a weekly schedule for the main performing groups in the school is to schedule the band, chorus, and orchestra first. Working with the guidance counselor and administration will help you in dealing with school conflicts. Do not leave the process of scheduling up to the administration or guidance departments, or you might very well find your very best student not able to schedule music for a semester. Class schedulers do not always know which students are strategic to the program; do not leave it up to chance. Work with those whose primary responsibility is to schedule all students in the school system.

Scheduling the music groups before other classes does not mean putting too much emphasis on the music department. Because of the cross-representational aspect of the student registration, it becomes a necessity to put all the music students together regardless of the school year. Once this is done, other classes that tend to be more homogeneous in nature can be scheduled around the music courses.

Usually, there is more than one period of major classes offered. For instance, there are often several sections of senior English or junior History. Thus, students can be put into other sections if their band or chorus participation conflicts with one of them.

Scheduling Music Classes and Electives

If your department offers classes such as music theory, history, theater, or other core or elective classes, you may be faced with a problem of scheduling and staffing. Often a department will consist of two or three (or fewer) music faculty who have schedules that are already full without additional electives to teach.

Many teachers will simply give up, claiming there just isn't time to teach electives and classes in music. However, *it can be done.* Figure 3-1 shows a suggested plan for establishing a music major program and a fine arts major program. Using existing staff with a minimum of additional funds, the major program can be implemented in most high schools.

The plan in Figure 3-1 can be implemented fairly easily if you keep a few things in mind. First, teach the courses on an alternate year basis. Second, teach only two courses per semester or year. Finally, make many of the courses one semester (one-half year) long. In so doing, two full-time music teachers can teach the classes and fulfill the three-credit requirement. The sequence will include grades nine through twelve.

The important thing in the scheduling of alternate-year classes and most electives is the length of the class term. Some core requirements and major ensembles should be one year long. However, others can easily be adapted to a Monday through Friday 20-week schedule, or one semester each.

Music Major

Requirements: 3 credits, including one from each of the classifications

I. Core Curricular Requirements (Musical Knowledge)
   1. Theory I or II
   2. Music history
   3. Conducting
   4. Composition and arranging

II. Skill Development Requirements
   1. Instrumental (band)
      (lessons and participation in a major ensemble)
   2. Vocal (chorus)
      (performing group plus instruction)
   3. Keyboard (ensemble)
      (performing group plus instruction)

III. Attitude Development
   1. American music history
   2. Folk music
   3. Guitar
   4. American musical theater
   5. Electronic music

Fine Arts Major

Requirements: 3 credits, including one from each of the classifications

I. Art, Art History or the Humanities
   1. Art
   2. Art history
   3. Introduction to the humanities
   4. Dance, theater (or drama) class, music theater workshop

II. Core Curricular Requirements (Musical Knowledge)
   1. Music theory I or II
   2. Music history
   3. Conducting
   4. Composition and arranging

III. Humanities Course or Performing Arts
   1. Humanities course
   2. Music skill performing course

Figure 3-1

Cooperating with Other Departments and Staff Members

Many times there are jealousies and resentments between the music department and other areas in the school. The music department "takes students out of classes for lessons"; it has high visibility within the school and community; and it often has a bigger budget (caused by the tremendous expense of music equipment). However, there need not be these conflicts within the school—or at least these conflicts can be minimized with a little effort and effective use of public relations. A mistake many music teachers make is to assume that public relations deals only with the music department and the community. But in a correct sense, the public becomes all persons or organizations not directly connected with the department. Therefore, teachers, administrators, nonteaching school staff, custodians, and all others who come in contact with your program also become the "public" with whom you should make every effort to establish a departmental relations program.

This may seem obvious, but it is often overlooked. Yet it can be one of your greatest assets in the school. Friendly, cooperative relations with the staff members are highly desirable, and there are ways to help alleviate normal tensions found between departments. First, remember to communicate. When you print your lesson schedule, rehearsal times, or proposed activities that may take your students out of classes, notify the teachers with a memo stating that you are trying to avoid conflicts. However, let the teachers know that they can come to you if a problem arises between their classes and your program.

Remember also to reciprocate with other departments. Let students miss a lesson or rehearsal occasionally if they are having a problem with other classes. Also, let the other teachers know you are doing this so they can understand you are trying to meet them halfway.

Finally, cooperate. This word is often taken for granted and not really put to use. But any system requires cooperation to run smoothly. Your willingness to cooperate with other departments who also have legitimate problems will help make it possible for them to cooperate with you. Keep in mind:

1. communicate
2. reciprocate
3. cooperate

Enlisting Administrative and Guidance Help and Support

In many schools, it is difficult to get full cooperation from the guidance and administrative departments, because they really do not understand the problems of music education in the public schools. Yet they are responsible for assigning students to the music classes. They are often important in steering students to vocational guidance. Therefore, it is important for you to help them become aware of certain unique problems in music and to enlist their help in maintaining continuity in the program.

Emphasize to them that performing groups are built over long periods of time, and that sudden or frequent changes in personnel do not help the department and should be avoided. Below is a list of concepts that should be given to your guidance department as information priorities. In other words, make it your project to let them know about your needs.

1. Older, more experienced students need to be kept in the program.
2. Strategic musicians in certain sections cannot be removed without hurting the entire group.
3. Music cannot be eliminated from a student's schedule one semester and put back in later without hurting the student's personal attainment and contribution.
4. Without an active "feeding" system to replace graduates, the program will deteriorate.
5. Music programs are built through *continuity*. When this is disturbed, the program suffers.

Keep up a good relationship with the guidance department and administration. They can be a real help in keeping *continuity* in your program. Use them and work *with* them. It will be worth it.

Using Students to Facilitate Rehearsals

Many band, chorus, and orchestra directors try to attend single-handedly to all the numerous details and tasks required in rehearsals. This method is time consuming and completely unnecessary. I strongly advocate the delegating of responsibilities to students and training them to take care of many details so that you are free to concentrate on the music. There are many areas that can be left up to the students to control *effectively*:

1. tuning with an electronic tuner
2. setting up chairs, stands, and music
3. inspecting uniforms or concert attire
4. calling late students
5. distributing programs
6. lining up properly for entering the stage

Many of these details can be assigned to student leaders. Not only will this free you to concentrate on more important things, it will also enhance the self-esteem of those who are in charge of certain details. Remember, students can do it, so be patient, let them learn, and get out of the way. Don't try to be in charge of everything.

Using the Open Ensemble

Many directors of large performing groups are so insistent on regular in-school rehearsal scheduling that they fail to take advantage of another alternative that can actually be a help to the program. This is the "open" ensemble concept.[1] The group schedules one or more rehearsals after school where students can meet informally to practice. The object of the open rehearsal is that it is open to any students who wish to participate. Some may not have had regular formal music study but are interested in music. This is the time and place where they might come and experiment, trying an instrument or their voices to see if this might be something they wish to pursue.

Scheduling this informal rehearsal after school helps to avoid students' signing up for a course they may not wish to continue once they have had a chance to find out what it's like. At the same time, some students may develop an interest in the group and a desire to pursue study further. They can then be channeled into the regular school curriculum and pursue formal study.

In addition to the possible recruitment of new students, the open rehearsal can act as a good time to help the regular students and a chance to have another "extra" rehearsal. Keep in mind, though, that this time should *not* be considered merely another regular rehearsal. The main emphasis should be on experimenting, extra help, and recruiting. It should also not be a requirement for regular group participation, but an option for those who wish to take extra time. Perhaps lighter popular music could be emphasized here to help attract students.

The open rehearsal concept can be a definite plus to your program in the following ways:

1. to provide adequate in-school rehearsal time
2. to recruit new students
3. to give extra help for sectionals and individual parts
4. to help students transfer from one instrument to another and gain familiarity with the new instrument
5. to find time to play lighter or popular music to use for special occasions

It is often true that most music teachers do not take enough advantage of opportunities to interest others in the art of music. It is not enough just to recruit the usual students at the beginning of each year. An ongoing and outgoing program should also try continually to attract new students. It may be a little inconvenient for you to attempt to schedule them, but it should be done. Musical interest does not just occur in September. *Experience in music* should be our aim with our teaching, and we must make every attempt to let *all* have this experience. As Professor Brand Blanshard has said:

> We are not a phlegmatic people; our feelings are strong and quickly inflammable. It is a widespread belief among us that if an experience is exciting, that in itself is enough to justify it and make it significant.[2]

Using "Informal" Teaching As an Answer to Scheduling Problems

In the event that certain students cannot be scheduled for specific lesson or instruction times, it may still be possible for you to retain them as productive music students. This might be accomplished by establishing another kind of informal schedule and teaching time. In other words, you would publish a list of those times when you will be free during the day and in the music room. Students then should be encouraged to come during their free time or study periods if they so desire. They can practice, use the music suite resources, or ask you for help. This informal setting can provide a relaxed and efficient use of both the students' and your time.

The setting up of this type of available department resources is not the answer to all scheduling problems, but it can be advantageous in achieving some continuity with instruction for those students who would not be able to study music otherwise.

Certainly you can, at least, set up a designated area in the music suite where students can come to practice their instruments. If you do not have a regular practice room, set up some section of the department that can be used as the regular "practice area." If the room or area can be large enough to include a piano, try to do so. This will give both keyboard and vocal students an incentive to come and practice.

One word of caution: Do not allow students to come if you or another music teacher cannot be there in the department. Should damage, accidents, or even personal injury occur, it can be a serious problem. Make sure that someone in authority is there any time students come to the music room.

Using the Computer to Facilitate Scheduling

A computer can be a real help in scheduling students and classes. Often there will be a central or regional educational center that will have the facilities to house and finance a computer. If you are able to request the use of it, it is often extremely beneficial to run through some programs. As Anthony G. Oettinger and Sema Marks have said:

> A computer is potentially an excellent tool for scheduling anything including itself, provided we tell it how. Like good tutors who can marshall resources beyond their own, computers can marshall most other educational devices and make them perform at their command, provided we have told them what to command.[3]

Thus, if you properly program a computer, it can sort and identify countless students and schedule them quickly and efficiently. As a result, you can review several possible schedules and adopt the most practical one in very little time. The computer, as an aid in speed and efficiency, can be of great benefit to you, the guidance department, and the administration.

Minimizing Conflicts between Performing Groups

Each chorus, band, or orchestra director will generally want to have as many rehearsal times per week as possible. Ideally, most would want five days a week. However, if a school is relatively small and each group meets in separate periods, a top-heavy music schedule may result at the expense of other courses. For instance, here is a nonconflicting schedule within the music department:

Period 1: Band
Period 2: Chorus
Period 3: Orchestra
Period 4: Class
Period 5: Class
Period 6: Class
Period 7: Class
Period 8: Study hall

A quick look at this reveals that only four academic classes can be easily scheduled. A fifth could be scheduled by eliminating study hall. However, the student will have a very tight schedule to follow, with very little free time. In addition, the student's day may be disproportionately high in music classes (a three to four ratio). Many administrators and guidance counselors would disagree with such a schedule.

If each group were scheduled simultaneously, it would free two more periods for courses. However, this would be done at the expense of making the students choose between groups. One solution to the foregoing problems is alternate scheduling, with each group meeting on opposite days (see Figure 3-2).

Schedule 1

	Monday	*Tuesday*	*Wednesday*	*Thursday*	*Friday*
Period 1	Band	Chorus	Band	Chorus	Band
Period 2	Chorus	Orchestra	Orchestra	Orchestra	Ensembles

Schedule 2

	Monday	*Tuesday*	*Wednesday*	*Thursday*	*Friday*
Period 1	Band	Chorus	Band	Chorus	Band/Chorus

Figure 3-2

Each director will sacrifice some rehearsal time, but will avoid conflicting schedules within the department. Each student could, theoretically, participate in all available ensembles. Three rehearsals per week is actually quite adequate if planned and run efficiently. More important, perhaps, is the fact that relations with other departments in the school would not be harmed by a schedule that may appear to be top-heavy with music classes.

Avoiding Problems with Private Lessons in School

Most instrumental or vocal lesson schedules are so tight that classes must be taught in small or large groups, rather than as individual lessons. Of course, private lessons are recommended for maximum achievement. Indeed, all music students should be encouraged to take private lessons from the best instructor available to them.

One problem that can occur in a school situation, and one that a music teacher should be aware of, is private lessons given in school for a fee. There does not seem to be a consistency in policy among different school districts regarding this. But a teacher giving lessons privately for money on school property—even if after school—can be a problem.

If your plans are to teach at school after hours, two things should definitely be done. First, secure permission from the school authorities, stating when you will be teaching. It is not necessary to discuss specific fees to be charged, but rather to get permission to teach and charge fees. Second, do not discriminate as to the availability of your services. Do not allow only *certain* students to study with you. Make it known that any who wish can take lessons. Indeed, as Richard Weerts states:

> Private lessons (on school time and property) are very difficult to defend unless they are made available to all students—or at least all students who desire them. The band (or other) director places himself in a particularly vulnerable position when he receives financial remuneration for private lessons he gives in school facilities–even if the lessons are not given during the actual school day.[4]

CHAPTER 3 ENDNOTES

1. The original idea was conceived by Wayne R. Jipson and described in his book, *The High School Vocal Music Program* (West Nyack, NY: Parker Publishing Co., 1972).

2. Blanshard, Brand. *The Uses of a Liberal Education*. LaSalle, IL: Open Court Publishing Co., 1973, 85.

3. Oettinger, Anthony G., and Sema Marks. *Run, Computer, Run*. Cambridge, MA: Harvard University Press, 1969, 53.

4. Weerts, Richard. *Handbook of Rehearsal Techniques for the High School Band*. West Nyack, NY: Parker Publishing Co., 1976, 71.

Chapter 4

Effective Rehearsals and Good Concert Programming

An ongoing problem most school music directors face is trying to prepare groups adequately for concerts and other public performances. Lack of adequate rehearsal time, missing students, and schedule conflicts often frustrate the director. In addition, directors are faced with concert programming concerns. Is the music right for the audience? Is it teaching anything to the students? Is it the type the individual director relates to, or is it over the heads of all and not uplifting to anyone?

These considerations become important as music directors face the urgent demands of a fast-paced school year, with varied audiences, student tastes, and the requisites of the school administration as to their perceptions of what school music should be like. Can rehearsals be a time of efficient teaching and practicing? Can public performances both elevate and entertain audiences?

The answer is "yes." A little care and some preparation ahead of time can improve your concerts and speed up learning in your rehearsals. In fact, it *is* possible to do some teaching in each rehearsal and still accomplish much in the way of learning new music. This chapter offers some practical advice and helpful tips to the preceding considerations.

HOW TO BUDGET REHEARSAL TIME EFFECTIVELY

One of the biggest problems that band, chorus, and orchestra directors face is how to accomplish one's goals in the allotted rehearsal time. The major complaint is *too little time.* The often-heard remark is "if we only had a few more rehearsals." School music directors seem to be nearly universal in this real dilemma.

The lack of adequate time or number of rehearsals is a problem that has not been limited to school music groups alone. Indeed, many professional and college directors vent the same complaint. It has been my experience to view this problem both from a professional performing viewpoint and a school one. It has also been my observation that, although more time can be beneficial, there is also the factor of much wasted time that seems evident in rehearsals. I have always been interested, from a professional orchestral musician's perspective, in the way that conductors use their rehearsal times. In fact, I have noticed that as we would play for a succession of guest conductors, there would be a great variance in the observed use of rehearsal times. From competent, efficient, and concise rehearsals, we would see the scale go all the way down to barely getting through the music. Yet each conductor thought he had the *best* method for accomplishing his goals.

It was both amusing *and* frustrating to watch some conductors use their time in a most ineffective manner. Respect toward the conductor from the players did not always relate to any inspired interpretive aspects, but rather to whether or not the director would waste time in rehearsals or keep moving efficiently through the major areas of need. Nothing was worse than sitting there bored while a conductor laboriously worked over a passage that should be taken care of some other time.

The same holds true for school music directors. Using rehearsal time effectively is much more important than adding extra rehearsals. Therefore, *budgeting* rehearsal time is of paramount importance. An excellent method for executing a program of rehearsal efficiency is to write a scheduled listing of numbers to be rehearsed, time allotted for each number, specific sections to go over (and times allowed for them), warmups or chorales to play, and specific announcements. Then *stick to the schedule*! Force yourself to follow it for a few rehearsals. It can be an eye-opener. You will discover where you tend to work too long in certain passages. You will learn just how quickly you can get an idea across, and where you may be lacking in rehearsal technique. The last one may hurt, but it will also help you to improve greatly, if you face it honestly. A sample schedule to follow is shown in Figure 4-1.

The previous example could be modified for any type of chorus, band, or orchestra. Individual modifications of time can be scheduled according to selections to be rehearsed, total time available, general level of student experience, and difficulty of works to be performed. But, again, the important thing is that some sort of schedule be followed.

Band directors often disregard the relatively little rehearsal time allowed for professional symphony orchestras. They say, "They are professionals and do not need as much time as my school orchestra." But band directors often fail to take into account the additional pressure involved when considering the level of musicality toward which these groups are expected to perform. Let's examine a typical weekly schedule.

Rehearsal Time Chart—2:00–2:50 PM

2:00–2:05 ....Students assemble instruments, etc.
2:05–2:09 ....Time, warm up chorale
2:09–2:13 ....Technique book—short exercise
2:14–2:18 ...."Matador"—John Cacavas
—new selection *read through*
2:20–2:40 ...."Russian Sailor's Dance"—Gliere
—for next concert
–ten minutes #5
#9
#14
–five minutes–beginning through #5
–five minutes–entire selection (put together)
2:40–2:50 ...."That's Entertainment"—Gilman
—for next concert
–five minutes—beginning through #33
–five minutes—#33–#66

Figure 4-1

The New York Philharmonic Symphony Orchestra has followed a basic schedule similar to this one:

	Rehearsal *a.m.*	*p.m.*	*Concert* *evening*
Monday			
Tuesday	rehearsal		concert
Wednesday			
Thursday	rehearsal		concert
Friday	rehearsal	concert	
Saturday			concert
Sunday			

In the previous schedule, the orchestra is rehearsing for the following week's concert schedule. Usually a total of three rehearsals are allowed per concert series. The four concerts listed are the same (the regular subscription series). Extra concerts, festivals, benefits, recording sessions, rehearsals, and children's concerts are not included. However, usually only one rehearsal is scheduled for these "extra" events.

In other words, each new regular concert program receives a maximum of three rehearsals (2 ½ hours each); every extra concert receives one rehearsal. The musicians are expected to *know* the music before they come to rehearsal. The conductor's job is to put it together. The schedule certainly is concise, narrow, and minimal. But within this program, much glorious and superb music is prepared and performed.

Thus, it would seem reasonable that with approximately three rehearsals per week and three months between concerts, a high school performing group would have sufficient rehearsal time.

One of the best articles I have read on rehearsal time problems is "If I Only Had Less Rehearsal Time" by Donn Laurence Mills.[1] In this short, thought-provoking piece, the author describes the average school orchestra director's preparation for concerts. He points out three basic stages of rehearsal time over a period of months:

1. excitement and interest because the music is new.
2. a plateau when interest lags and the concert time has not yet come near.
3. a period of intense concentration and accomplishment just before the concert.

Mr. Mills points out that much of stage two is not used for any real accomplishment, but becomes merely repetition. However, in a situation where few rehearsals were scheduled near the concert and high expectations were instilled, students accomplished much in a short period of time. Mr. Mills suggests, as already recommended, that you "lay out rehearsal plans by the minute, not the hour."[2]

COPING WITH MISSING STUDENTS IN REHEARSALS

It is sometimes difficult to get many rehearsals where all students are present. Illnesses, early dismissals, special programs, conflicts in schedules, and many other reasons may keep students out. Concentrate on helping those students who *are* there, instead of worrying about those who aren't. If the first chair player in a section is absent, use the time to help the others gain confidence in their own playing and lean less on the section leader. In other words, take a positive approach. Work towards improving the quality of those players who are actually in rehearsal. Those who are not will likely make enough rehearsals to learn the music well, although it sometimes is necessary to make a minimum number of rehearsals a requirement for playing or singing in the group.

PUNCTUALITY AND ITS IMPORTANCE IN REHEARSALS

Most public school systems operate on a bell or buzzer system. Therefore, the end of the rehearsal is not usually a problem. Rehearsals usually end three or four minutes before the bell rings, thus giving students time to put their instruments or music away. It is at the beginning of the rehearsal that problems in punctuality can emerge.

After the bell rings to begin the rehearsal, most directors allow students five minutes or so to get out their instruments or music, warm up, and generally get ready to rehearse. But, human nature being as it is, most students (and adults for that matter) will take the maximum accepted time to begin. If the director isn't careful, or is preoccupied with administrative concerns, it will sometimes take ten or more minutes for students to get in their places. Most of the time is wasted.

The solution is to set a maximum amount of "get ready" time and a precise moment when rehearsal will begin. Announce this to the students, and then *stick* to it. Start your first rehearsals when so stated, even if 50 percent of the students aren't there yet. Let the latecomers know that you mean business. It will not take long for students to hurry along and be on time.

Be fair, however. Allow students *enough* time to get ready and warm up as shown here. But excessive time is a waste and makes for inefficient rehearsals.

Beginning Rehearsal-Time Schedule

1. Bell Rings	10:00 a.m.
2. Students Enter Rehearsal Room	10:03
3. Students Warm Up	10:03–10:08
4. Rehearsal Begins	10:08 PROMPT

GROUP INSTRUMENTAL WARM-UPS

An interesting way to play scales is in ensemble sections rather than all together in unison or octaves. One method that helps promote more group and sectional individuality is the scale in chords as a three-part style:

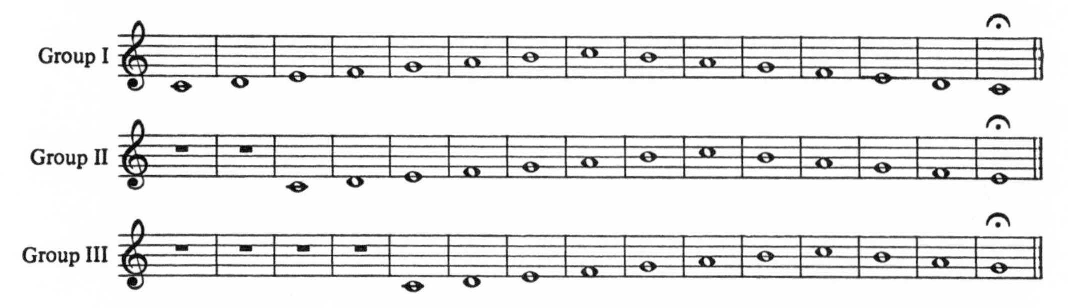

In addition to creating a certain independent level within sections, this is a tremendous exercise for developing controlled intonation.

Another exercise that can be used as a warm-up and help in intonation and blending is the following, which is appropriate for any instrumental combination:

Chords and scales develop basic fundamentals in large ensembles; they are especially important in blending and intonation. Many similar exercises can be developed with only a minimum of preparation.

GROUP VOCAL WARM-UPS

While most choral directors have favorite warm-up techniques that may have been passed down from their teachers, many are also looking for new and different ones to add variety to what is an important but often boring part of a choral rehearsal. Exercises that are effective have a specific area that will need improving and become helped by doing. Some emphasize the general warming up of the voice; others concentrate on a specific technique such as tone, intonation, blending, vocal technique, or range.

Some examples of short, fast, yet effective, warm-up techniques include the following. The first is a vowels warm-up; the second, a light, fast technique.

In other words, use the regular vowel sounds with the preceding consonant usage of N, M, L, K, or T. Follow the pattern upwards until you feel the choir's effective range has been reached.

With both exercises, it is best to do them two or three different ways: First, sing them legato and nonarticulated; next, use some form of syllable, such as la, na, or some open-type vowel with any consonant. Follow this with the actual solfege symbols since this greatly faciliates the learning of the solfege and is alo an enjoyable way to do it.

By singing them legato and articulated, the group will be warming up in two different areas. First, the legato uses the open throat nonarticulated sounds that will warm up one set of muscles. Next, the articulated sounds will warm up still another set of muscles. Vocalists often overlook this aspect that is similar to a wind instrument technique. Tongued notes use one set of muscles while slurred ones use something else. It is not within the scope of this book to get involved with the physiological aspects of musical production, but perhaps it would suffice to say that the above statements are true. And whether one knows about the muscles in the oral cavity or not, one can "feel" these muscles at work.

Here is a third exercise that can be used as a general warm-up:

Syllables: La, Lee, Lo, Lu
Nu, Nee, No, Nu
Ka, Kee, Ko, Ku
etc.

The above exercises, both vocal and instrumental, are certainly not meant to be all-inclusive. You can and should add many of your own creative touches to warm-up drills. However, by keeping them short and specific, you can accomplish much in a short period of time. The students will usually find the above "fun" to do, and in the high school or junior high situation, "fun" can be the difference between an enthusiastic, highly motivated group or a large drop-out rate.

The last two exercises especially will improve diction, and the choir will be "ready to sing with clean clear diction." Tone quality and diction are inexorably linked together. One will enhance or detract from the other—*your emphasis* on these will produce the results. Simple, easily prepared exercises similar to the above will produce results.

USING SECTIONAL REHEARSALS AS A VALUABLE LEARNING TOOL

Learning difficult passages or tricky ensemble playing is something that can be taught in sectional rehearsals. This will allow the whole-group rehearsal to be used for everyone, and you won't have to waste a section's time while you concentrate on just one group. Sectionals are relatively easy to schedule, because as a concert or performance time draws near, you can put the sectional groups in the regular weekly lesson schedule and rotate them. This will usually entail your losing one week of regular lessons. But it will not greatly hinder the program since the students will still be learning. And the lost lesson time should be gradually made up during the regularly scheduled lessons after the concert.

Sometimes students in a section may be available to hold a sectional, but your own schedule will not free you to be there. This would be the time to let the *section leaders* handle the rehearsal. It will allow the group to rehearse and let the leaders gain experience in exerting their leadership.

HOW TO REHEARSE INDIVIDUAL SELECTIONS FOR MAXIMUM LEARNING

Along with the general outline of the rehearsal itself, there are some effective ways to get the most out of rehearsing individual selections. Referring to Figure 4-1, we can observe how much time might be spent on each selection as a whole. But how do you use this subdivision of time for its most efficient accomplishment?

As a general rule, rehearsing compositions in three stages during one rehearsal works quite well. First, read through the entire selection, if it is not too long. If it *is* too long or difficult, read at least one main section of the composition. Next, isolate and concentrate on the problem areas. Last, try to put the section together again as a whole. Simple, yet effective, this method should speed up your rehearsal time.

So keep in mind:

1. Read through.
2. Isolate and concentrate on problem areas.
3. Put together as a whole.

If you are working with young students, you will want to put together the entire composition as often as you can. I have been in groups that never actually played through the entire composition until the performance itself. This can be a rather harrowing experience for all involved, even yourself. The group will sound different when the whole composition is played or sung. And it is sometimes doubtful as to the chances of the group getting through the whole piece unless they have had *much experience* doing it. Endurance and concentration are two things involved in a composition that cannot be tested until you actually go through the entire work.

HOW TO KEEP A RECORD OF REHEARSAL PLANS

Earlier we discussed how to budget rehearsal time with a chart, showing time limits for each selection. Within that basic time structure, you can keep a worksheet, describing specific places in the music that need attention. This record does not have to be elaborate or formal. Simply keep an account, on a sheet of paper, of rehearsal plans for each day.

You could include on this sheet the title of the selection, the measure numbers of problem areas, and the reason for difficulties in that selection. Try to follow your schedule for the most efficient rehearsing possible and the least wasted time:

Selection "Highlights from Camelot"

1. Work over—letter A thru C (especially 3rd Clarinets 5 after 13)
2. Work on brass intonation—letter G thru H
3. Spacing of notes needs attention—final five chords

HOW TO PROGRAM MUSIC FOR MAXIMUM AUDIENCE RESPONSE

Symphony orchestras and other professional groups spend a lot of time presenting important and beautifully prepared compositions. However, after their rehearsal preparations are complete, they do not simply bunch the selections together and play them until they are done. In fact, a great deal of thought goes into the program order of selections. The basic reason for this is to calculate and bring the maximum audience response. After all, if the audience remains interested from the beginning to the end of a composition, they are likely to come again.

Public school performances should also be designed for the probable response from the audience. Do they like the music? I recently had a conversation with a band director who had a very good ensemble and did some noteworthy compositions. But he was discouraged by the lack of audience enthusiasm and appreciation for the work that the group put into their rehearsals. He said that, on one recent concert where they performed a transcription by a serious composer, the group worked extremely hard and achieved much in the way of musical results. At the end of the performance—the apparent culmination of months of hard work and serious rehearsing—the director expected, at the very least, a standing ovation. When the audience gave only routine and uninspired applause, he was shocked and discouraged.

Perhaps the reason for this lack of positive response had much to do with the programming of the music. Directors often face three distinct and important areas of audience and performer tastes:

1. the players or singers
2. the general audience
3. the administration's understanding

Music directors usually have a highly developed understanding and appreciation for the deeper or heavier concert music. The audience may range from real music lovers and performers to those whose appreciation of art in general is a peripheral aspect of their lives. The administration will usually have some preconceived ideas about the music and what a school group should be like.

Faced with these diverse tastes and expectations, it is quite difficult to present music that everyone will be able to appreciate. One possible solution might be to offer a wide variety of music on the program, so that each group will be able to appreciate *something*. Another important part of the solution is to program the music so that the audience can relate to your group from the first.

Many concerts have what I refer to as a gap between the performers and the listeners:

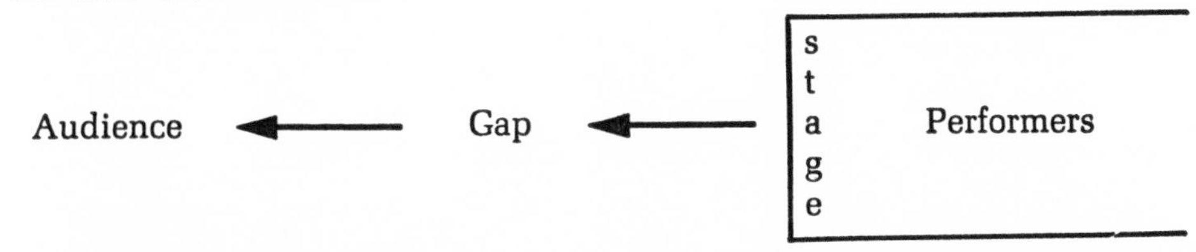

This is psychological, yet it is very often real. There is a lack of empathy established between the two groups.

The best way to begin some sort of connection is to announce a few selections, or to tell something about the music or performers. Just a few words will often break the ice. The audience will have a connection between you and the first row of people.

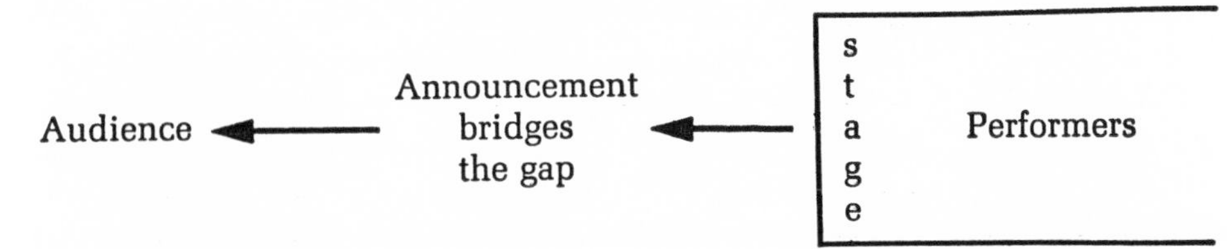

The music itself should be programmed, as has already been mentioned, to *help* the audience relate and appreciate. Think in terms of the following:

1. an "opener"
2. settling in
3. something different
4. a "closer"

The four points above, although simplistic, can really help in audience response. An example of a symphony concert might be the following:

1. overture
2. symphony or concerto
   —intermission—
3. contemporary or lesser known work
4. lighter selection

Translated into an actual concert, the above might mean:

1. Overture "La Forza Del Destino"—Verdi
2. Symphony No. 5—Beethoven
   —Intermission—
3. "Verklarte Nacht" (Transfigured Night)—Schoenberg
4. "Tales from the Vienna Woods"—J. Strauss

The program listed above contains the four basic elements of a good program. The overture should be recognized as flashy and fast moving—a good transition from the audience's outside life to their concert life. The Beethoven Symphony No. 5 is popular and keeps the audience interested immediately after the overture.

After intermission, Arnold Schoenberg's Transfigured Night is played. Depending on the sophistication of the audience, this work may not be very familiar to many. Putting it in the first half of the concert, or even at the very beginning, would not be a good opener. Its subdued mood, "heavy" meaning, and difficulties are not conducive to effect the transition from outside to inside (concert life). But programming it after a couple of familiar selections should make the audience listen. After this lesser known piece is the "closer," something that may make the audience leave whistling your music.

The above suggestions have been done, have proven effective, and are taken seriously by those who wish to exert maximum audience response. In fact, the broadcast industry even codifies selections to be played on the air, so that certain coded works will be used at the right time—before the news, in the middle of the broadcast, and so on.[3] They do not take chances. Instead, they utilize whatever knowledge they may have about each piece, and program it selectively.

The Importance of Good Audience Response

It is important that audiences relate to the music, because you want them to attend your concerts; you want them to enjoy the concerts—not to come just because their sons or daughters are performing. Therefore, research your basic audience. In each community, audiences are different. Are the majority of parents well educated, are they "country and western" oriented, or are they "classical" in tastes? The level of musical appreciation they bring to your concerts is the level at which you should start.

The key phrase in the preceding paragraph is "the level at which you should *start*." Begin at the audience's general level, and gradually attempt to broaden their tastes. But don't try to do it all at once. Rather, take them through music appreciation slowly. You, as a local music teacher, can help teach the parents as well as their children. Subtly, you can help them increase their musical interest by following the program order suggested.

The opener and closer should be on their level. Rather than play music which may be very far above their heads, attempt to increase their understanding by taking one step at a time. It may not be exactly the music you desire, but if it pleases the audience, it will help your program. Above all, try to program some music that will entertain. It does not have to be humorous, but some type of lighter music will help. The audience should respond positively.

USING A WIDE VARIETY OF MUSIC FOR EFFECTIVE TEACHING

Every music teacher will bring to his or her performing group a unique set of tastes, interests, and prejudices. As a result, there may be a tendency to stay close to one type of music. It may be Broadway musicals, the classics, jazz, or popular. But the important thing to remember is that every student in the group will have, or is developing, a unique set of interests also. Therefore, it is your job to help these students develop an appreciation for various types of good music, and let their own tastes grow gradually. In addition, as music educators, our responsibilities are to teach *all* types of good music.

Therefore, it becomes important to expose our students to as many different types of music as possible. We must subordinate our own tastes and reach out to a more cosmopolitan program, so that the various interests of the students will be allowed to grow.

In addition, when taking our audiences into account, it is also important that they hear a variety of music to suit their own individual tastes. Don't try to please everyone. You can't! But do offer them all a choice.

Sometimes a program of only one type of music can be rather dull. I remember attending a state music conference once and going to hear the guest performing groups one evening. The first group was a wind ensemble from a college with a very high reputation. The ensemble played an entire program of avant-garde music. No traditional sounds were heard; only innovative, unusual techniques were heard. The audience response became more and more subdued as the program continued.

The group following the wind ensemble was a college orchestra, which opened with an overture by one of the Romantic Era composers. The change in music was like a breath of fresh air. One could see the audience visibly perk up and respond positively. A standing ovation was given this group after its program. This was not just because of the fine job done, but also because of the variety this group offered as compared to the first group. There was nothing wrong with the music of the wind ensemble. It was simply the perceived unrelenting sameness of the music that bored the audience and made them wish for variety.

Therefore, be aware of the needs, wishes, and tastes of your audience. Reaching them will help in your public relations. And you will have a feeling of accomplishment not often sensed in public school music.

SCHEDULING FOR THE ENTIRE YEAR

Concluding your preparations, rehearsal methods, programming, and presenting concerts, one thing more needs to be done. During each year, make tentative plans for the following year. As the semester progresses, you may have ideas for the things that you would like to do. Write them down as possibilities for the following year. This will help you effectively plan each year's goals, objectives, and desires.

At the end of one year you will probably have listed numerous ideas. These will be your starting point in developing future plans. By writing these down, you will be able to remember them. If you do your planning during the summer months, this list of ideas will give you concrete suggestions.

By planning your entire year's schedule, at least in some outline form, you will be able to see if your overall program is making progress and developing smoothly. Music directors, who plan only from one concert to another, will not be able to easily see if the entire music program is achieving its goals. Planning *is* important, and it should be done steadily and thoughtfully.

CHAPTER 4 ENDNOTES

1. Mills, Donn Laurence. "If I Only Had Less Rehearsal Time." *The Instrumentalist,* January 1981, 82.

2. *Ibid.,* 83.

3. Kinney, Guy. "Concert Programming: Tips from the Broadcast Industry." *Music Educators Journal,* December 1978, 45.

Chapter 5

How to Effectively Stage Assemblies, Concerts, Community Programs, and Other Musical Presentations

Musicians are trained to make music. Music educators are trained to teach music. Not all, however, are trained to organize, develop, and administrate the various ways to present this music to the public. Many teachers become most anxious and nervous just before concert time, trying to wrap up the last-minute details that must be taken care of and finished.

All types of public performances have different and important matters that must be organized in order to deliver a smooth presentation. These can range from securing ushers, stage help, lighting, and programs, to getting custodial help and administrative permissions. How does one solve all these details, and do it simply, without forgetting some important aspect?

This chapter will make your task an easy and complete one. Checklists, planning ideas, and other tips are presented to facilitate all types of programs. These are all tried and tested. They have been proven successful and should be valuable aides for you.

HOW TO ORGANIZE PROGRAMS FOR COMMUNITY GROUPS

Whenever you are asked to give a music presentation to a community group, you must consider whether the program is indoors or outdoors. If if is the latter, then acoustical considerations will include the following: Do we need amplication in order to be heard, or will the audience be close enough so that they can hear us easily? If, however, the program is to be presented indoors, then you will immediately want to know what type of room or auditorium will be used. A small room with a low ceiling will have entirely different acoustics than a large, high-ceilinged room.

Vocal, string, wind, or percussion ensembles need different physical surroundings in order to sound best. Check these out personally, if possible, because you can usually tell what a room is going to be like merely by snapping your fingers.

Once you have an idea of the acoustical properties of the room, you can then plan the music accordingly. Music should fit the room. An acoustically "dead" room will not enhance the sound of a brass quintet, or anything else. On the other hand, a hall with "live" acoustics will add to the sound of an antiphonal choir doing Renaissance music. Common sense should prevail, and you will be able to program accordingly if you personally see the room in advance.

Another consideration, which may be the most important one, will be to program music that will fit your prospective audience. You can usually obtain some idea about the audience when you first speak to the person in charge of your presentation. A concert of "heavy" serious music may not work for a lodge or community group that always has "light" or popular music for its functions. It will not be a compromise to your goals if you present music that will please them. Good public relations include meeting the needs of your audience, and you should attempt to do this. Indeed, this is your function. Community support will be the reward.

Some other details that you should first take care of include the following:

1. Who is the person in charge of securing your group?
2. Will that person introduce you? Or will someone else do it? Or is that up to you?
3. Are programs needed?
   a. Who does them?
   b. Who *pays* for them?
4. Who will provide transportation?
5. How long will your presentation be?
6. If the group is paid, where do funds go?
   a. Group's own fund?
   b. School music account?
   c. School general account?
   d. Other?
7. Will there be any room(s) available for warm-ups, changing clothes, and other details?
8. Will the organization hold a meeting immediately after your presentation? If so, will your group be able to leave or stay during it?

All of the above questions should be answered as soon as you begin making arrangements with the person in charge. Surprises as to what is expected of your group at the program are not welcome. You should know all these items right away. Sometimes parents meet their children after the program. It certainly would be nice for them to know what time this would be. Public relations are *not* enhanced if the parents must wait a considerable amount of time for their children.

Mailing Publicity Announcements

Publicity is important to a music program for two very good reasons:

1. It lets the public know when musical events are going to be held.
2. It is good public relations to know that the music department is active in the community.

The public media, which includes newspapers, radio, television, and other means, can be utilized more than most music departments use them. In fact, some very good media events go by without the public being aware. Often this is caused by a music director being unsure of just how to write a good news release or where to send it.

However, this is a fairly easy task if the basics of good news reporting are adhered to. The news media want to know certain things that all reporters seek: *Who? What? When? Where? Why?* Therefore, if you keep these in mind, you can write any news release easily without worrying about trying to compose a piece of literary prose. Keep it simple and to the point (see Figure 5-1).

The details presented in Figure 5-1 are really all that is needed to get an announcement across. Beyond this you can explain the highlights of the program, the selections in detail, and other pertinent information. The more you include that is interesting or different, the more likely the media will use it. Do not simply list the selections to be performed. That is the purpose of programs. But include the highlights, theme, or different selections to give the reader an idea of what to expect.

The news release is not an essay, a philosophy of the music department (although you can write an article about this for a newspaper at an appropriate time, but not as a news release), or a chronological listing of selections. As a detective would say, "just the facts."

A radio release is written the same as a newspaper release. However, because television is a visual medium, a regular news release will usually be used only on the stations' community announcement features. If you want real coverage, you would have to have the television cameras come and tape some event.

Name of Organization ______________________ Date ______

Name of Director ______________________ Release Date ______

Name of Person Writing This ______________________

1. *Who*
The Regional Elementary School Band under the direction of
2. *What* 3. *When*
Mr. Guy Kinney will present a concert on March 12
4. *Where*
in the school auditorium. The concert will celebrate the

"Irish Spirit" as exemplified by the approaching St.
5. *Why*
Patrick's Day.

Figure 5-1

HOW TO MAKE IN-SCHOOL ASSEMBLIES SUCCESSFUL

One problem that many directors of school groups face is the apparent lack of appreciation of their group by the general student body or faculty in their school. This can be doubly disturbing if they have the opportunity of giving an in-school assembly and are faced with the fact that the students basically did not enjoy it. This problem can be resolved by doing one essential thing: *Program and gear the music to the level of the audience.*

I recall one band director who told me that he no longer plays for the students because they do not like his programs. A few words about his concerts, however, revealed that, although the ensemble performed admirably, the music was way above the heads of most of the student body. The remedy would be to find out what the students like, and base the program on their findings. It would not be wrong to try to raise their understanding of music, but this should be done gradually. The same concept of gearing music to the general audience also goes for the students. They will enjoy your assembly if you play or sing music that they can relate to and enjoy.

Recently, some state music groups played at the state capital for a public relations concert for the legislators. Some people complained that the ensembles programmed lighter or popular music, instead of performing the hardest, most serious music in order to impress the lawmakers. However, by presenting music on a lighter scale, they delighted the state legislators, most of whom were not very knowledgeable about classical or serious music. But they loved what they could understand, and they *understood* what they heard! Public relations were made in a positive successful manner. The concert was a resounding success!

Your relations with the student body and other faculty members can be made stronger if you present music that relates to them. If they enjoy the music, they will like your group; make an attempt to reach them.

The Importance of Organizational Details

One important aspect of an in-school assembly, that is often overlooked, is timing the program to fit the assembly's allotted time. Schools are regulated by time. If the regular program of the school day is to accomplish its goals, each course and teacher needs a scheduled amount of time. A special assembly will usually disturb this schedule. Therefore, in order to minimize the disruption, it becomes important for you to schedule your assembly with accuracy. Time the length of each selection and the announcement (if any), and try to stay within those bounds.

Another important item to account for in staging an in-school assembly is the amount of time it takes for the general student body to come into the auditorium or the place where the program is to be held. Sometimes, it can take as long as fifteen minutes for all the students to enter and sit down (every school is different). But you cannot easily begin the program until all have arrived. So, if you schedule a one-hour program, but fifteen minutes is used up in audience arrival time, then your whole program will be cut short. Therefore, *account* for this arrival time.

You will also need time for music students to arrive before the concert begins. They may need to change clothes (if required) or to warm up their instruments or voices. Allow enough time for this, but don't take too long. You do not want the students to become bored and restless while waiting to start the program.

If your program uses any special or tricky lighting or stage arrangements, make sure someone is appointed to take care of these. You should not have to do these yourself. Rather, concentrate on the substance of the program, and let someone else be responsible for the logistics of your concert.

So, keep in mind:

- student body arrival time
- musicians' arrival and warm-up time
- length of program
- responsible assistant for lights, curtains, and other details

Achieving Cooperation with Other School Personnel

As already mentioned, if you can stick to an accurate schedule, and if other teachers know this schedule, you will minimize disturbances to the regular school schedule. Most teachers welcome an occasional assembly for their students. But they can become rightly frustrated when planned class time is unexpectedly cut and disrupted. Therefore, the first aspect of faculty cooperation will be to let them know far enough in advance of your program, and tell them the correct times of the program.

It is also important that you do not overdo the frequency of your program. Too much of anything can be bad. Try to hold a few assemblies each year. Try to make the audience want more music and not leave feeling they had too much. This is very important to remember. You love music; most musicians can practically "eat, sleep, and live music" but the average nonmusician does not love music *that* much.

HOW TO PREPARE FOR EVENING CONCERTS IN SCHOOL

As with in-school assemblies, there are certain things that should be done to insure a smooth performance. These details are simple, yet important, and they can make your job much easier. One thing that is often overlooked when music directors prepare for night concerts, is a method to check on missing members. It is quite possible that student or two might become ill from the time school ended in the afternoon to the time of the performance. If you have to drop the immediate details leading to the concert and make telephone calls to find out why Johnny Smith isn't at the school, it can be most disconcerting as well as frustrating.

Therefore, make it a practice to designate one student whom other students should call in case of illness or emergencies. That student should also be supplied with a list of telephone numbers of all the members, so that he or she can call to find out information. Should you feel that you have no student who could do the job, ask a parent to assume that responsibility. As simple as this task may seem, it can relieve you of a burden and allow you to concentrate on more important matters.

Some other details you should plan well in advance are shown in Figure 5-2. Item 7 in the Checklist is very important because much good music is lost after a concert due to the students' feeling that it is no longer needed. Collect, account for, and store music in a specific place to prevent losing it.

A checklist is essential, in order for you to know that everything is being done. Any form of list will do, from the simple one listed in Figure 5-2 to a more complicated one. Some very good suggestions for checklists are found in Kenneth Neidig's book, *Music Director's Complete Handbook of Forms.*[1]

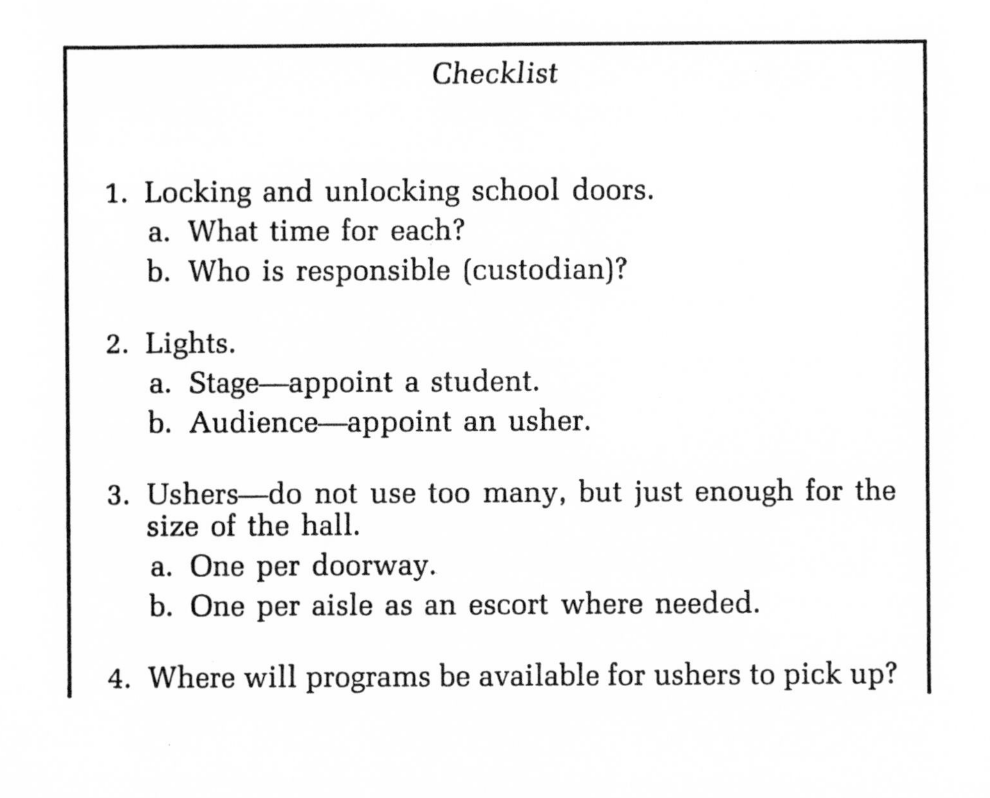

Checklist

1. Locking and unlocking school doors.
   a. What time for each?
   b. Who is responsible (custodian)?

2. Lights.
   a. Stage—appoint a student.
   b. Audience—appoint an usher.

3. Ushers—do not use too many, but just enough for the size of the hall.
   a. One per doorway.
   b. One per aisle as an escort where needed.

4. Where will programs be available for ushers to pick up?

5. Complete programs in plenty of time for printers to finish and return to you.

6. Warm-up time for the ensemble.

7. Where do students leave music after the program?

8. Appoint or solicit volunteers to act as stage managers:
   a. Set up chairs.
   b. Arrange stage.
   c. Take down risers or chairs after intermission starts, and similar details.

9. Time the entire program.
   a. Parents like to know when their child will be home.
   b. If program is too long, it will lose the attention of the audience.

10. Publicity—find a chairperson to handle this:
    a. Newsletters to media.
    b. Posters.
    c. Announcements.

11. Are tickets to be given, or is there to be a charge?
    a. Who prints tickets?
    b. Who is box office person?
    c. Where does money go?

Figure 5-2

Making the Program Meaningful

Quite often, establishing some identifiable theme to the program will enable the audience to understand and relate to your presentations. It does not have to be anything fancy, but just some sort of thread that those attending the performance can recognize. In other words, rather than programming a random list of selections, try to make some sort of connection between them. This connection may be quite thin, but even this can be helpful. Below is a list of themes that often apply to school programs of performing groups:

"A Tribute to the Classics"
"American Music"
"Music for Everybody"
"A Choral Chronology"
"Contemporary Tunes"
"Toe-Tapping Tunes"
"Broadway Tribute"
"Marches on the March"
"Christmas Around the World"
"Classics with a Tune"

The possibilities are numerous, and selecting a theme is worth investigating. Audiences appreciate knowing what you are trying to accomplish in your program. They are also entertained when they understand your efforts.

How to Simplify Charging Fees for Concerts

Some schools regularly charge fees for school concerts and performances; others never do. Here are some helpful ideas to make the job easier, if fees are charged.

Earlier we discussed public relations as they apply to in-school cooperation among the faculty and staff members. If you are charging a fee for your concerts, one thing that you can do to enhance the above is to give complimentary tickets to faculty members. Most likely not enough faculty will take advantage of this offer to reduce ticket sales greatly. But even so, you will gain so much in the way of positive feelings between the music staff and the general faculty that it will surpass any lost revenues. This simple gesture is well worth the effort.

Once you have decided on ticket sales, you can reduce your costs by using simple one-color tickets from construction paper. However, if the program is repeated on more than one night, you might use different colors for each night. Simply cut out the paper to correct size and use each color as an identifying ticket. Of course, elaborate tickets can be printed, but they may be costly, and you may rather use homemade ones.

AVOIDING POTENTIAL PROBLEMS WHEN PERFORMING RELIGIOUS MUSIC

In a school situation you will probably have students from many different faiths. During the school year most music departments present Christmas concerts and Easter programs. Thus, you may face the problem that certain religious works may offend those with differing beliefs. At the same time, there may be strong popular sentiment to present the traditional music of the season.

Performing the seasonal religious music need not be discontinued if you consider certain things. First, when you perform music that may conflict with others' beliefs, concentrate on the beauty of the work, not the textual meaning. Certain recognized works are of such stature that they are accepted for their musical and artistic worth by most persons. Examples include "Messiah" by Handel, "Jesu Joy of Men's Desiring" by Bach, and "A Mighty Fortress Is Our God" by Luther.

Selections of major works like these are generally recognized as works that are accepted for their music. However, specific hymns from a particular church's point of view, which may not contain the accompanying musical value, should probably not be performed as these may offend someone.

Basically, you will need to use common sense. Don't cause unnecessary disagreements over the music used. Stay with the accepted and musically important. At the same time, however, try not to be closed-minded about a new or untried work just because it may be religious. Perhaps it is significant in its musical value, so that the music outweighs the religious viewpoint. Use your own judgment.

HOW TO GET THE MOST COOPERATION FROM YOUR STUDENTS

Music directors often find it difficult to realize that students may not value music at the same high level that they do. In fact, directors have a tendency to think that something is wrong with the students if they have a less-than-ideal love for their ensemble. While most students usually do care about the groups to which they belong, these feelings do not necessarily dominate their whole lives.

Hence, it is important that we accept this fact and view our job not as the most important aspect of the students' lives. This will help us all keep a proper perspective and not make undue demands on students. Too many extra rehearsals, or even too many performances, may cause weariness in some students and even a wish to be free of a growing burden on their time.

While you should not settle for less in your musical goals, remember to settle for fewer rehearsals and shorter times. (Remember that even professional ensembles stick to a carefully timed rehearsal because there is usually an enormous penalty to pay in overtime expenses.) These may prolong the student's enjoyment, which is more important than your drive for perfection. I have seen band directors who expect an unwarranted number of evening and Saturday rehearsals, choral conductors who do not understand the outward limits of endlessly long rehearsals, and orchestra leaders whose penchant for sectional rehearsals causes the players to wonder if it is worth it. Don't overdo your influence! Stick to a strict schedule. Let the students know when rehearsals will begin, and when they will be over—and then follow this time carefully.

Student groups should rehearse in order to learn and concerts should be a culmination of that learning. When students give a public performance, keep that in mind and make the performance enjoyable for your students. They are not professional musicians, and should not be expected to perform as such.

PERFORMING FOR COMMUNITY, POLITICAL, AND RELIGIOUS EVENTS

It is always a matter of pride to have the local school groups take part in official community functions. If precaution is taken not to overdo it, such events can help build morale in your groups. And participation may help public relations. In addition, the school, as a public institution, should be willing to take part, since this will add to the general education of the students.

Political Events

One word of caution regarding political events is in order. If your group performs at a program, speech, or meeting which is purely political, you could be running the risk of some unforeseen problems. The opposition could accuse you of favoritism. Also, they could demand equal time or representation, leaving you caught in the middle.

Therefore, be careful whenever you are asked to do something at a political event.

Religious Events

The same caution and consideration should be taken whenever your group performs for a specific religious event. You could run the risk of criticism, which may claim that you favor a certain church or church group. If you do perform in or for a church, try to do it fairly and be available for other groups as well. Generally, community services, which include all local faiths, create a climate where you can participate safely.

Store Openings and Other Related Events

Public, private, and college school groups should be careful about participating at "grand openings" of stores or any other event that could be considered basically commerical in nature. The main concern is the concept of *professional* versus *amateur* in the performing group. The ethics involved are complicated, but the International Musician's Union views professional music in a serious protective state. While not wanting to interfere with school or other amateur groups, it does wish to protect the employment possibilities of union musicians.

Commercial establishments, on the other hand, are often willing to let school groups perform free rather than pay for professionals. It is not the intent of this book to preach the ethics, legalities, or rights of either group. But you should think carefully about whether your ensemble is interfering with professionals.

HOW TO SCHEDULE CONCERTS FOR INEXPERIENCED GROUPS

An inexperienced group will not perform as well at a concert as a highly polished ensemble that performs often. Even if you have rehearsed long and hard, certain unexpected things may tend to "throw" the group. For instance, if lights should not work correctly, or if someone makes a mistake, students may panic. A selection could suffer or fall apart. Where the experienced group should be able to overlook the unusual occurrence and continue when it happens, the inexperienced ensemble will not usually be so adaptable.

Of course, the only way groups become experienced is to go through these trials and tribulations of public performance. The best preparation you can make for your students' confidence is to discuss with them those unexpected things that can happen during a concert, and caution them to try to ignore mistakes; prepare them for the unexpected.

CONTINUING MOTIVATION OF ADVANCED GROUPS

No matter how exciting or enjoyable something might be, it will tend to become routine with repetition. I can remember my days studying privately with the Principal French Hornist of the New York Philharmonic. My lessons were given at Philharmonic (Avery Fisher) Hall. My teacher used to talk about scheduling my lessons down "at work." This struck me as totally incongruous, since playing with such an an orchestra at such an exciting place could not possibly be considered "at work"! Nevertheless, after years at his job, he did not see it as glamorous.

The point, however, is that you need to motivate and be motivated in order to continue to progress and accomplish something better or new. Your high school music groups can seem routine, and even boring, to the students, if they continue to do the same things over and over. The secret to keeping boredom from affecting the group's morale, attitude, and performance is to do something new from time to time. Don't let your rehearsals or performances become too routine. Change things at regular intervals. Do something new or different to break the monotony of too much repetition. Sometimes this should be done even at the expense of necessary rehearsal time. It may greatly improve student morale.

DOING SMALL CLASSROOM PRESENTATIONS

Whenever you take a small group into the classroom, two things should immediately be considered. First, since this is not a concert stage, you should encourage a sense of informality. Do not try to present a formal concert. Instead, capitalize on the informality that is probably already there. Use informal remarks, discussion, question-and-answer techniques, or any other presentation methods to encourage informality.

Another important thing to remember is that, since you will apparently have a captive audience, do not make your program too long! Keep it short, and keep it interesting. Long, drawn-out descriptions of the music, or extended periods between selections, will lead to restlessness in the audience. However, if the program is short, the audience (even if they do not necessarily like it) will usually be patient and attentive.

CHAPTER 5 ENDNOTES

1. Neidig, Kenneth L. *Music Director's Complete Handbook of Forms.* West Nyack, NY: Parker Publishing Co., 1973.

Chapter 6

Special Projects and Music Activities That Can Be Done in Class, After School and at Home

Many aspects of the school music program do not fit in directly with the school curriculum. These activities come under the heading of special projects. Included may be after-school and at-home small ensemble rehearsals, instrumental repair classes, school musicals, special class decorations for a specific unit of study, teaching the "business" end of music, and many others.

Understanding the importance of the occasional special project in motivation and the various methods for initiating it easily will help your planning and can make your job easier. This chapter relates those methods that have proven beneficial and effective in the school situation.

HOW TO DEVELOP SMALL ENSEMBLES THAT CAN REHEARSE AT HOME

Music teachers often argue that one of the values of music study is that it can be used at home as well as in school. But do we actually provide many opportunities for students to make music at home? Of course, there is usually the expectation of at-home practicing, but I am referring to an actual music-making effort, especially with others. The making of music as an enjoyable and informal activity outside the school should be encouraged.

The creation of informal small ensembles can be an answer to this dilemma. Students can be grouped into small sections where the distance (at home) between them is not great. Next, supply them with lighter or popular music in which they may have an interest. Should you find that the group doesn't fit a standard, prescribed ensemble format, form an "uncommon" ensemble and arrange the music accordingly.[1] Do not worry about balancing the parts or blending. Rather, let the students have fun and experiment as they go. They should be encouraged to play for themselves, for their own enjoyment, not necessarily for a concert performance.

USING STUDENT "COACHES" AFTER SCHOOL

Normally, whenever two or more people come together to make music, some leadership is needed. During the school day, you will provide that essential as the teacher. However, when you establish informal groups of instrumental or vocal students, you may not be able to attend their rehearsals. It is, therefore, a good idea to appoint one student whom you deem to have the necessary source of responsibility to act as the group's "coach." Don't call that person a teacher, but rather refer to him or her as "Coach." Coaching the group is less formal than teaching them!

Tasks provided by the student coaches may include distributing and collecting music, setting tempos setting cut-offs, scheduling rehearsals, and generally keeping things moving and in order. Students will usually react positively towards a peer who tries conscientiously to carry out those duties, but they will tend to be negative towards one who tries to "fill" the role of the regular teacher. So be sure that you appoint the right kind of student coach.

THE AFTER-SCHOOL INSTRUMENT REPAIR CLASS

There are many music students whose talent to perform on a musical instrument is very marginal. At the same time, some of those same students take apart an instrument and put it back together almost better than it was originally. They do have "musical" talents, but not necessarily in the same sense that we normally assume. They need to be able to use them.

A factor in much of today's economic climate that inhibits the easy flow of money into school music departments is that fewer and fewer new instruments seem to be purchased at any one time. As a result, schools are increasingly turning to repairing their instruments in order to reap maximum benefit from their investment. However, even the costs of repairing instruments can greatly deplete a budgeted item. An alternative to the high costs of new instruments and professional repairs is to initiate an instrumental repair class.

Students who have a high mechancial aptitude for this will enjoy learning about and actually doing instrumental repair work. The question, however, is: How does one learn about instrumental repair, and how complicated is it? Instrumental repair can be quite simple and quick; it can also develop into a highly polished and time-consuming craftsmanship. Assuming you lean toward the former, and many of us do, instrument repair can be a quick, easy, and expedient way to save money and keep instruments in playing condition.

As far as repair methods are concerned, there are four basic methods for learning:

1. Take a formal instrument repair class at a college.
2. Study as an apprentice with a trained instrument repairman.
3. Study some of the published materials on instrument repair independently.
4. Figure it out for yourself.

The last method was not put there to be facetious. Many fine and adept persons can figure out simple repairs as well as any trained repairman. However, before trying this method, make sure it is *the* correct way to fix something by checking with a person who knows the acceptable methods. I can still remember, painfully, the young student who had an expensive trumpet mouthpiece (almost brand new) with horrendous gouges carved into it by an overzealous father who used a wrench to "unstick" it from the trumpet.

The third method listed is recommended as a relatively painless and thorough way to learn instrument repair. Some fine materials have been published, listing various sources that explain the step-by-step process of repairing the most common needs. These articles usually explain all tools and equipment needed to do the job. Each task is taught as a step-by-step process for the person who has no background at all in instrument repair.

One such method is the book *The Practical Band Instrument Repair Manual.*[2] Written in a clear, precise style, this text is supplemented by clear and concise illustrations. Not meant to be a treatise on complicated instrument construction, it is, instead, a quick way to fix the most common breaks, bends, and distortions that instrumental teachers see on a regular basis. This manual is in spiral notebook format, which makes it easy to lay on a table, to stand against a wall, or to hold while you put information into practice.

In addition, numerous articles have been written about *practical* instrument repair. Some of these are listed at the end of this chapter. They would be worth pursuing to obtain copies. Various instrument makers also publish, from time to time, instrument-maintenance brochures that give directions for routine repairs. check with your dealer or service representative for information regarding these.

Once you have mastered certain levels of rudimentary repair work, you might then start to teach the techniques to a small class of interested students. Relying on a student to fix a broken pad or bent key is more convenient than having to give up part of your rehearsal time when Sally Jones accidentally drops her clarinet. Schedule your class at a time convenient for those who are interested. Often, an after-school time is best, since it does not have the pressure of the in-school day's curriculum. In addition, an air of informality prevails, which helps the class to progress pleasantly.

Be prepared yourself, but do not attempt to teach the students those areas with which you are not familiar. Be willing to state that you do not know how to do something. Then research it, and return to the class with the answer. Students will respect this.

PLANNING A SCHOOL MUSICAL AS AN EDUCATIONAL ACTIVITY

For most students, faculty, and audiences, a presentation of a musical is lots of fun—time-consuming, sometimes frustrating, but still fun! On the other hand, it can also be an *educational endeavor*. Rather than simply starting rehearsals, it can be a real help if you first give some background about the work. For instance, I remember reading an article by Alan J. Lerner about the difficulties he and Frederick Loewe had trying to convert Shaw's "Pygmalion" into "My Fair Lady." The author discusses the very real difficulties involved in adapting a prose work into a musical. Students can get an understanding of the art of writing such a work, as well as producing and acting in it.

Knowing the temper of the times in which the work was written, and whether the composer was trying to make a sociological comment or expressing a specific opinion can also be helpful. The problems of ethnic diversity in "Fiddler on the Roof," or justice in "Camelot," or moral fidelity in "Damn Yankees" are subjects that can be discussed, even though the main thrust of most musicals is pure entertainment.

No matter how you do it, the important thing is that you do present some sort of historical and social background before you begin production. The presentation of musical theater should be enjoyable and inspirational, but it should also be educational. The musical should be included as part of your music program curriculum. Wayne R. Jipson lists the following reasons for doing musicals:

1. The musical is, and has been, an accepted part of our culture since the beginning of the Twentieth Century. To ignore it is neither realistic nor fair to our students.
2. Contrary to the beliefs of many, the musical can be done with emphasis on musical values.
3. The musical can serve as the perfect bridge for the often discussed generation gap. The music contains many aspects of both "classical" and "pop" writings.
4. The musical can be a catalyst for the entire music department. It can create an enthusiastic drive for a common goal throughout our entire school.
5. The musical will serve to draw into the choral program students who might otherwise not become involved. The teacher then has the opportunity to broaden their musical horizons.
6. If the director handles it correctly, the musical can be kept in proper perspective in relation to the rest of the choral program.[3]

Coordinating Production and Making the Rehearsals Run Smoothly

In order to reduce the frustration, rising tempers, and setbacks that often accompany in-school theatrical productions, designating a production coordinator is a good idea. This person should be someone (other than yourself) who will be responsible for making sure that each committee does its job efficiently and does not overlap with another. Each chairperson reports to this coordinator. This then frees you, as the director, to concentrate on the main aspects of the production. The coordinator's job is a simple one, if the entire staff understands from the beginning how the show will be run.

The task of each committee and committee member will be made easier if each knows where the lines of communications go and who to report to. The coordinator will report to you, so that only general planning will be your responsibility. The details will be implemented through this person (see Figure 6-1.)

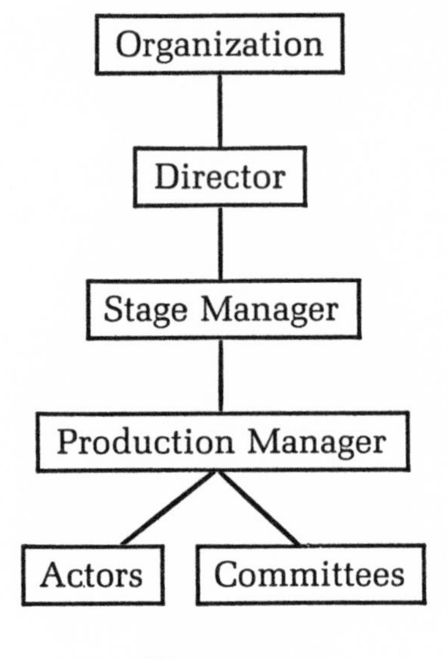

Figure 6-1

Planning the Rehearsal Schedule Efficiently

As a professional performing musician whose contributions to musical theater have been limited mostly to the pit orchestra, I can appreciate the difficulties in trying to accomplish specific goals at rehearsals. I also can understand the frustrations of the director and the need to "do it until we get it right." When this need gives way to long rehearsal times over the regular schedule, it can cause two problems:

1. spending too much money—in the professional world
2. making unreasonable demands on the students' time in school

We should never make demands on students' time over and above that which we originally told them about when we started. This should hold true *even* at the expense of some unmet rehearsal objectives. In the professional world, I expect to be paid for a certain length of service. The schedule will be run according to the pricing regulations of the musician's union and hiring contractor. When the rehearsal ends on time, it is because of money.

However, some of my greatest respect goes to those amateur directors to whom I have volunteered services. Those who have stuck to a schedule, begun and stopped *on time*, and did not call for extra rehearsals have my deepest respect, because their integrity as to concerns for the time of the volunteer cast is high. On the other hand, the opposite is true about those few productions with which I have worked where directors casually started an hour late and ended *two hours* late! There is no excuse for this. Only in a *real* emergency should you extend your rehearsal demands on the students' time.

Therefore, you should plan (block) the entire rehearsal and production schedule from the first auditions to the opening night. Some of the most careful considerations of all must go into this. The schedule should be neither too long nor too short. Rather, it should be concise and sufficient to gradually lead to a heightened interest and smoothly operating opening night. Figure 6-2 is an example of a good school or community schedule, remembering that the members of the cast are volunteering their time.

TEACHING THE "BUSINESS" OF MUSIC

As music educators, we are most often concerned with the outward manifestations of our art, learning music and performing it. Too often, however, we have not sufficiently educated our students about the business side of music. How do they make a living out of music? Should they choose to do so, what are the career opportunities available? What are the part-time or avocational possibilities? It is important that to discuss this with your students, so that they will be aware of the options.

The first things that come to mind are teaching or performing. But even here we should describe what a teaching position involves. What are the requirements? What would a performing career entail, and how difficult is it to obtain one?

Other areas that should be investigated include such things as:

instrument repair
instrument and music retailing
arranging
composing
recording production
criticism and literature
music and acting (musical theater)
conducting
church musician

Regional Elementary School Chorus
Rehearsal Schedule for "Annie, Get Your Gun"
Times: Tues & Thurs. 7:30–9:30, Sun. 8–10

	S	M	T	W	Th	F	S
JAN.	4 General Read Through	5	6 ACT I Scene 1-3	7	8 ACT I Scene 1-3	9	10
	11 ACT I Scene 1-3	12	13 ACT I Scene 1-3	14	15 ACT I Scene 1-3	16	17
	18 ACT I Scene 1-3 MEMORIZED	19	20 ACT I Scene 1-3	21	22 ACT I Scene 1-3	23	24
	25 ACT I Scene 4-6	26	27 ACT I Scene 4-6	28	29 ACT I Scene 4-6	30	31
FEB.	1 ACT I Scene 4-6	2	3 ACT I Scene 4-6	4	5 ACT I Scene 4-6	6	7
	8 ACT I Scene 4-6 MEMORIZED	9	10 ACT I Scene 4-6	11	12 ACT I Scene 4-6	13	14
	15 All of ACT I	16	17 All of ACT I	18	19 All of ACT I	20	21
	22 All of ACT I	23	24 All of ACT I	25	26 All of ACT I	27	28

Figure 6-2

This list can go on and on, but it should start you thinking along these lines. One way to teach these ideas to students is through a regular lesson plan making the opportunities practical.

A colleague of mine uses a very practical method for demonstrating various music jobs. In a music theory class, the students are told to write a simple composition (composer). Next they arrange this work for specific instruments (arranger) and write out the individual music parts (music copyist). Then they perform it with a director (professional musician and conductor), record it on a tape recorder (record producer), and pass the tape around the room (music retail business).

Many possible variations to the above can be imaginatively thought out and used in whatever direction you wish to take the students. The important thing, however, is that you *do* teach the students about opportunities for employment in music and music-related fields.

Often there are professionals in various musical fields living nearby who may be willing to come in and describe their work for your classes. This first-hand information is often the best way for students to really see what it is like to work in certain music-related occupations.

SCHOOL PROJECTS WITH SHORT PREPARATION TIMES

Many interesting projects can be done in the classroom as part of the regular curriculum, or as a supplementary learning tool. These can be used to maintain interest, increase motivation, and provide for personal application. An example of this might be a project called "Homemade Music."

This project involves the entire creative process, whether great or small. Students will write their own tunes, orchestrate or arrange them, and build the instruments on which to play them. This does not have to be a long, drawn-out, complicated project. You will be teaching the students the simple beginnings of the art of instrument construction. Do not let this last part scare you. You really need to know very little about any type of "building" to do this. By using your imagination you can "invent" all sorts of instruments. Students, especially those in grades seven and eight, usually enjoy working with their hands. (Caution: Be sure the tools are used by students only under adult supervision.)

Flutes

Simple homemade flutes can be made from lengths of garden hoses (see Figure 6-3). Materials needed are small-bore garden hose, corks of different sizes, small drill and bit (hand type), knife, and paint (for decorating).

Cut the garden hose into one-foot lengths, and drill holes for finger positions. Cut the blow hole with a sharp knife, and cork the end near the blow hole. Decorate with paint.

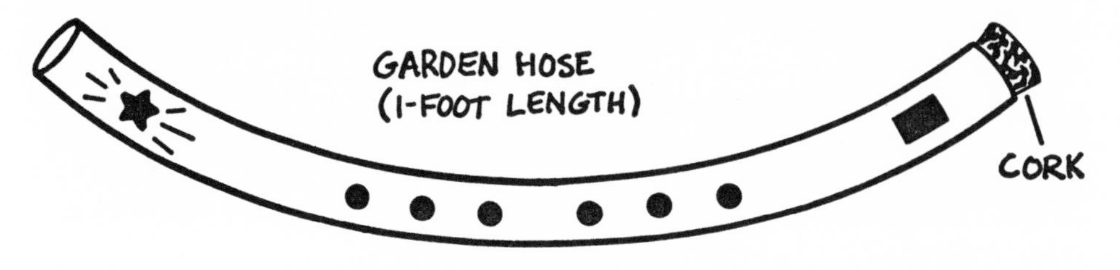

Figure 6-3

Drums

Coffee cans make nice drums. Materials needed are coffee cans of various sizes, an old inner tube, scissors, paint, sandpaper, wood dowel rods, small block of wood, circular saw, and hand drill and bit (see Figure 6-4).

For the mallet (drum beater), cut a hold in the center of a 2″ × 2″ block of wood with the drill and bit. Make the hole slightly smaller than the dowel rod. Cut the block with a circular saw to round it out,

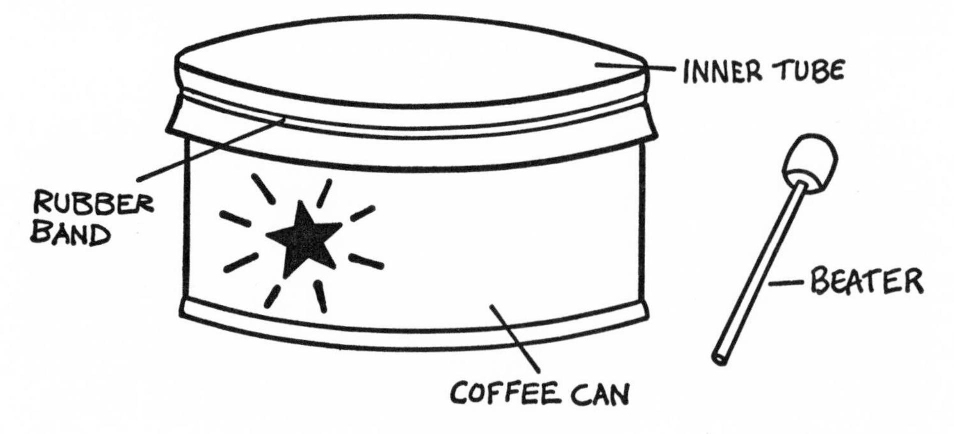

Figure 6-4

and taper the end of the dowel rod *slightly* with a saw. Pound the rod into the drilled hole and smooth the beater with sandpaper. Different-size cans will make drums with different timbres.

Stringed Instruments

Stringed instruments can be made with simple boxes and rubber bands. You will need boxes, knives (or scissors), rubber bands of various sizes and thicknesses, masking tape, and paint (see Figure 6-5).

Cover the box on top with cardboard and tightly tape all the ends. Make a slit in the box top towards one end and insert a long piece of stiff cardboard so that one end goes all the way to the bottom of the box. You may tape this to secure the "bridge" tightly. Cut small notches in the bridge for the "strings," as in Figure 6-6. Add rubber bands all the way around, paint to decorate. Tune the rubber bands by using different sizes.

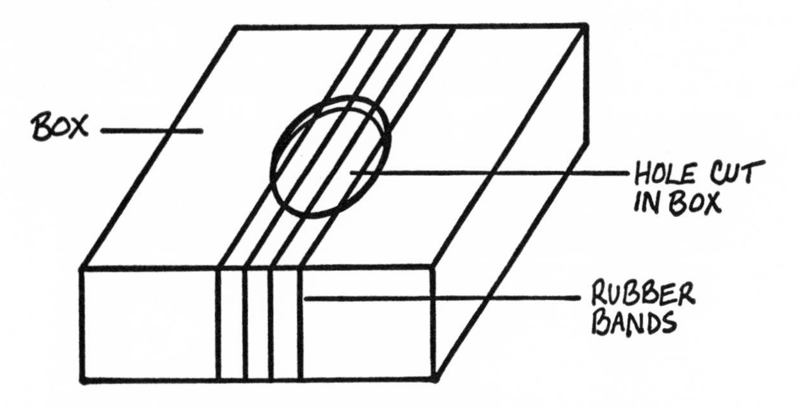

Figure 6-5

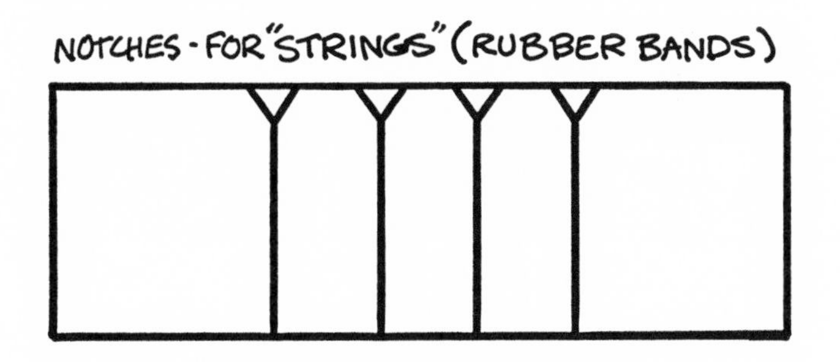

Figure 6-6

PREPARING FOR A "MINI-CONCERT"

In regular music lessons, students often work on solos of various types. Many of these are studied as a learning experience in their regular lessons. Public performance is not always the purpose. With the exception of solo and ensemble contests, most of the solos are played for the music teacher only. Yet I remember someone once telling me that a writer is only a writer if someone reads his or her work. And perhaps musicians need to play for others in order to develop their musical potential fully.

Public performance on a solo level builds confidence in a way that no other form of music can. It is one of the most effective methods of maturing young musicians. However, opportunities for this are usually few. Therefore, the "mini-concert" idea is a teaching technique that can be most successful. These concerts comprise an after-school recital series, whereby students who have learned solos can perform them in front of each other. The audience, generally small, fits the need of someone to play for and is mostly made up of those students who are waiting to play their own solos.

This small recital can be a fairly relaxed way of allowing the students to gain in confidence and grow in musicality. Included will be instrumentalists and vocalists as needed. Some teachers may wish to use programs, hold the concert in the auditorium, or may simply wish to have students sit in the class or rehearsal room in an informal manner. As formal or as informal as you may wish to do it, the mini-concert series is an effective outlet for students to use their talents.

CHAPTER 6 ENDNOTES

1. Kinney, Guy S. "The 'Uncommon Ensembles' and How to Make the Most of Them" in *Complete Guide to Teaching Small Ensembles in the High School.* West Nyack, NY: Parker Publishing Co., 1980.
2. Tiede, Clayton H. *The Practical Band Instrument Repair Manual.* Dubuque, IA: William C. Brown Co., 1970.
3. Jipson, Wayne R. *The High School Vocal Music Program.* West Nyack, NY: Parker Publishing Co., 1972, 171.

Chapter 7

Strategies for Keeping Interest in the General Music Class

There has been much recent debate as to the value of a general music class. Should the class continue to be part of the required curriculum, should it become an elective, or should it be discontinued? Certain schools seem to have problems with the class. Yet the class is so successful in other schools that there is really no question as to its validity.

Just why does this problem occur? Can it be resolved? Can we make a general music class a viable learning experience for all our students, and can it be made interesting? The answer is a resounding "Yes!" But the answer lies with the course content, the teacher's dedication, and, to some extent, the facilities and supplies available.

We must make every attempt to offer a course in which student interest will remain high, and for which respect will be included. It is significant, then, that we organize the course content to be relevant to the students. Strategies for keeping interest in the General Music Class must be a prime objective for organizing the course. Innovations—large and small—can be used to heighten interest. Such things as "catchy" names for units or projects, or team teaching with other departments, or personal involvement on the part of the students have proven successful. These can be a beginning. Many other possibilities are available. Planning is required, but the result can mean success.

WHY SOME GENERAL MUSIC CLASSES ARE NOT SUCCESSFUL

As a student in general music classes, I can remember how the teacher passed out workbooks. Each workbook had pages of composers' biographies in a short three- or four-paragraph synopsis. The composer's picture was included along with his story. At the bottom of the page were questions about the reading. Our task was to read the story and write out answers to the questions. This went on, day after day, with no discussion, audio-visual aids, or practical personal involvement— just reading, questions, and written answers. I can't remember anything about the biographies, but I do remember the pictures. I used to spend the time drawing beards, mustaches, and glasses on the faces. As I look back, I am not so sure that that mischief was all my fault! The teacher did not exactly motivate the class.

Too often general music classes are offered in this manner—matter of fact, uninteresting, and without real dedication. But it doesn't have to be that way. General music classes *can* be successful and interesting. It is the *way* the materials of music are presented, rather than the materials themselves, that will create or destroy interest.

THE IMPORTANCE OF GENERAL MUSIC CLASSES IN THE CURRICULUM

In *Secondary School Music*, the authors ascribe part of the importance of a General Music curriculum from grades K-12 as follows:

> General Music is the core of school music. It is that part of music education directed toward the needs and interests of all students from kindergarten through the senior year in high school.[1]

General music reaches students who may not be involved in the school performing groups or any other aspect of music participation. In fact, however, it may be one of their goals to be truly appreciators of music—the audience, the listener! These and other students have a need to be taught to understand, to discriminate, to identify skillfully various types of music, or to have a rudimentary knowledge of writing or arranging it.

Music is a subject, an art form and an everyday part of life about which students should have an opportunity to learn. But this learning should be done correctly, systematically and logically. In other words, a classroom or teaching setting is important for a comprehensive understanding of the skills necessary to discriminate in music.

BUILDING INTEREST IN THE PROGRAM WITH "CATCHY" CLASSES

It has already been pointed out that changing the name of some traditional music classes can also change the attitude of the students. For instance, "Homemade Music," which teaches rudimentary composition, theory, and performance, does what most music classes try to accomplish. However, the emphasis is on the *student* doing this and doing it *all*. Therefore, the interest is heightened because of personal involvement.

Many possibilities can be implemented to motivate students in your music classes by "creating" interesting classes that they will want to take. Some examples are listed below. The adroit reader will understand the thinking behind such titles.

"Homemade Music"
"Song Writing"
"Record Collecting"
"American Folk Music"
"The Age of the Pioneers"
or
"Pioneer Evenings"
"Stories of Music"

Many such titles may be used to attract the students' interest. Of course, they can be developed into solid courses with important content. Titles, such as "American Folk Music," "The Age of the Pioneers," or "Pioneer Evenings," can trace the development of early American music. "Record Collecting" can turn into a music appreciation class containing important facts about many different types of music. "Song Writing" obviously can be the beginnings of theory and composition. "Stories of Music" might include dramatic events in the lives of the great composers, etc. Each class can be developed to suit your own tastes, and each can attract students.

USING THE TEAM TEACHING APPROACH WITH OTHER DEPARTMENTS

Team teaching is a somewhat controversial approach to classroom teaching that seems to have passed its initial phase of enthusiasm. Yet, when done correctly, it can still be a valuable method to approach various units of the course from a different perspective. If you are teaching the mechanics and methods of brass instruments, why not use the expertise of a brass specialist in the school or a professional from the community? If you are discussing the harmonic series and the fundamental properties of a tone, rely on the information of the physics teacher. The Pythagorean experiments regarding the intervalic relationships of tones can be elaborated upon by the teacher of geometry.

In other words, the team teaching approach can be utilized as a supplement to enrich the class. This will greatly enhance student interest. When not overdone, team teaching can be a real asset to the class. Team teaching can be done within the music department and it can be done among other departments. It does take a little planning, but it is worth it.

Math and Music

You can help the students understand the basic relationships between intervals and their respective vibrations per second by asking the math teacher to come into your class to discuss ratios and proportions. The concepts that create the perfect fifth, for instance, can be explained by mathematics as demonstrated by the ratio of the octave versus the fifth. Pythagoras demonstrated this by the examination of a string. When stopping the string in the middle, he discovered a 2:1 ratio for octaves. Other intervals displayed different ratios and proportions. The math teacher can help explain these concepts.

In addition, it is possible for the explanations of meter signatures, note-value counting, proportions of triple versus double rhythms, and so on. Since there is so much math involved in all of this, the teacher will be able to show the close relationship that math and music are in.

Science and Music

The science teacher can be a very helpful and interesting person to help in team teaching. He or she will know the science of acoustics which is basic to how we perceive sound, timbres, and the nuances of music. For instance, what creates a bass sound, or tenor sound? In addition, the teacher can explain the fundamental system of tones and the harmonic series. Many high school science departments own an oscilloscope which can visibly demonstrate various sound waves.

The "how to" of electronic tuners, tuning forks, and sympathetic vibrations can be explained in an articulate manner by the science person. With you supplying the musical knowledge and the science teacher supplying the technical, your classes should prove interesting and informative.

Gym and Music

Most physical education teachers have a good understanding of the muscular and skeletal system that aids them in teaching the physical exercises that will help develop good coordination and healthy bodies. That teacher, thus, is a logical choice to help the music teacher work with creative dancing. He or she will know how to combine physical movements with dance steps that will enhance the movement of the body in rhythm.

There should not be the separation between physical education and music that there usually is. The two—dance movements and physical exercises—should be combined. Make use of the resources available in the gym classes for music and movement.

In addition, there has been much written on the subject of music and movement by Emile Dalcroze.[2] This eurythmic approach has been enthusiastically promoted for such things as:

understanding rhythm
dynamics
improvisation
composition

Indeed, Mr. Dalcroze's definitive work seems to state that all aspects of musical study and understanding can be helped by eurythmics. In so far as you incorporate these into your classes, you should avail yourself of the expertise of the physical education teacher.

Shop and Music

In our discussion about "Homemade Music," we talked about the building of simple musical instruments. More advanced construction techniques can be learned from the Industrial Arts teacher. He or she would be the one whose knowledge would extend to the building principles of most instrument construction.

Even if your goal was not to actually build instruments, the shop teacher would be used to help explain the ways instruments are put together. The forging, twisting, turning, and soldering required to make the brasses or the rounding, sanding, and smoothing of string instruments can be a most interesting discussion for your classes.

History and Music

History and music are closely related. The historical events of the world also influenced the arts, and composers generally reflected the feelings and attitudes of the people in their music. Even inventions and industrial progress were reflected in the music.

It, therefore, becomes very important that the cross relationships between historical, political, national, and international events be brought together in order that history might have a relevant meaning to all who study it. The person who can best help you in this will probably be the history or social studies teacher.

The expertise of his or her learning can be effectively used in a team teaching approach. Since music history and political history are interrelated, the two of you can bring together the interpretations that will be helpful in discerning the reasons for the art and culture of a specific era.

Too often there is no connection from one academic disciplinary area to another where history is connected. Yet all are intertwined to a certain extent. For instance, take a specific date and tie it internationally with other events. An example might be in the classical area:

Classical Period

1750–1820

French and Indian War	1754	Benjamin Franklin
American Revolution	1776	Franz J. Haydn
French Revolution	1789	Wolfgang A. Mozart
		Thomas Jefferson
		George Washington
		Frederick the Great
		Catherine the Great
War of 1812	1812	Napoleon

In other words, when Mozart was writing his exquisite music, many other things, of course, were going on in the world. Students, however, don't often correlate the cross currents of world history. Hence, when they study George Washington's accomplishments, they do not make the connection that Mozart was also alive. The history teacher can shed light on these world relationships and thus help the students comprehend the overall "world picture" for various musical eras.

Geography and Music

In many schools there is not a separate geography teacher or department from the social studies area. Basically all three, history, geography, and social studies, are combined. Yet the geography of a region or people should be emphasized in order to bring out the various cultural differences between countries and regions of the world.

Indeed, musical nationalism of the second half of the nineteenth century was a direct result of the cultural awareness of peoples of various countries and their unique points of view. Reasons for the social, economic, and political activities of a country are those things that a geography teacher can bring out and help students understand why the nationalistic composers sought to develop their special characteristic styles of music.

HOW TO SIMPLIFY THE TEACHING OF SYMPHONIC FORM

General music and music history students often have a certain amount of difficulty trying to understand symphonic form. This is usually because many or most of the students spend time with those types of music (i.e. popular) that do not have complicated thematic development. Or if they do, they are of such a different type that they do not readily correlate to the symphonic forms.

By simply outlining the formal structure, as in the example below, and following this with listening, students can get an idea of form fairly clearly.

Sonata—Allegro Form
(Introduction)
I Exposition
II Development
III Recapitulation
(Coda)

However, there is another way to demonstrate form that the students can understand and relate to quite easily. This includes the visual-analytical-aural approach. Simply put, this means looking at, listening to, and analyzing.

The example presented in Figures 7-1 through 7-9 is a lesson plan to teach the thematic development of symphonies by using the second movement of Beethoven's Symphony No. 8. Included are brief summaries of history, themes, formal structure, and orchestration.

Each page of the lesson plan can be set up as a page on the overhead projector or even as a slide. As you analyze, look at, and listen to the music, the students will all be able to follow the projected pages together.

HOW TO USE THE BULLETIN BOARD EFFECTIVELY

Bulletin boards have many potential uses: to reinforce present teaching, to supplement a unit with other materials of a different perspective, or to decorate the room. Some authorities have said that too much decoration tends to distract students from the teacher's discussions. However, others have said all available space should be utilized for course reinforcement.

You should strive for some sort of accommodation in between the above opinions. At any rate, some logical reasons exist for maintaining bulletin boards and there are ways to increase class interest and motivation effectively. Purposes of a bulletin board in teaching may include:

1. Teaching aids
2. Motivating a particular area
3. Summarizing work covered

In order to avoid the aforementioned criticism, you will need to evaluate your plans for the bulletin board material. The following questions should be answered carefully:

1. What is the purpose? Does it serve this purpose?
    a. How does it help in teaching?
2. Does it have variety?
    a. Do the colors contrast?
    b. Is the spacing adequate?

Visual-Analytical-Aural Approach

Symphony No. 8 in F, Op. 93. . . . Beethoven

Second Movement

Introduction:

Beethoven's Symphony No. 8 in F was composed as a result of an invention by his friend, Maelzel. Maelzel (pronounced Mats-zel) had just invented a mechanical device called a metronome. This invention ticked away a steady beat so that a performer could keep the rhythm steady. (see Figure 7-2).

When Maelzel showed this device to Beethoven, the composer spontaneously improvised a song on the piano. It made a joke of the metronome. However, later Beethoven took the song and used it in the second movement of the symphony.

This piece is the second movement of the symphony, and there are three other movements to it. Beethoven wrote *nine* symphonies altogether.

He also wrote string quartets, woodwind ensembles, concertos, choral works, and an opera.

Figure 7-1

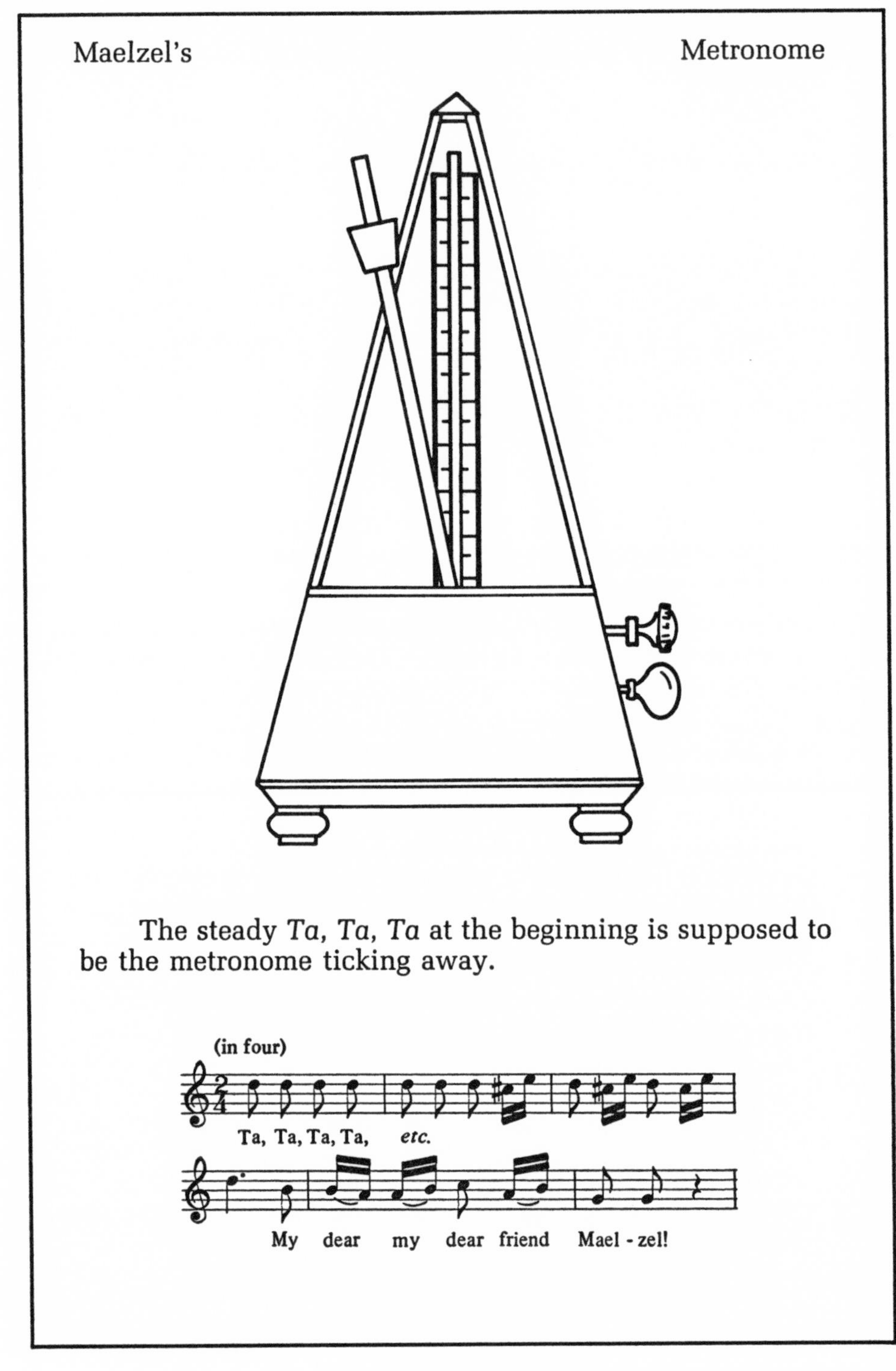
Maelzel's
Metronome
The steady *Ta, Ta, Ta* at the beginning is supposed to be the metronome ticking away.
(in four)
Ta, Ta, Ta, Ta, etc.
My dear my dear friend Mael - zel!

Figure 7-2

Form

Sonatina
Form

(sonateena)

A. Exposition (beginning and main themes)

B. Recapitulation (return to beginning)

C. Coda (tail or ending)

Figure 7-3

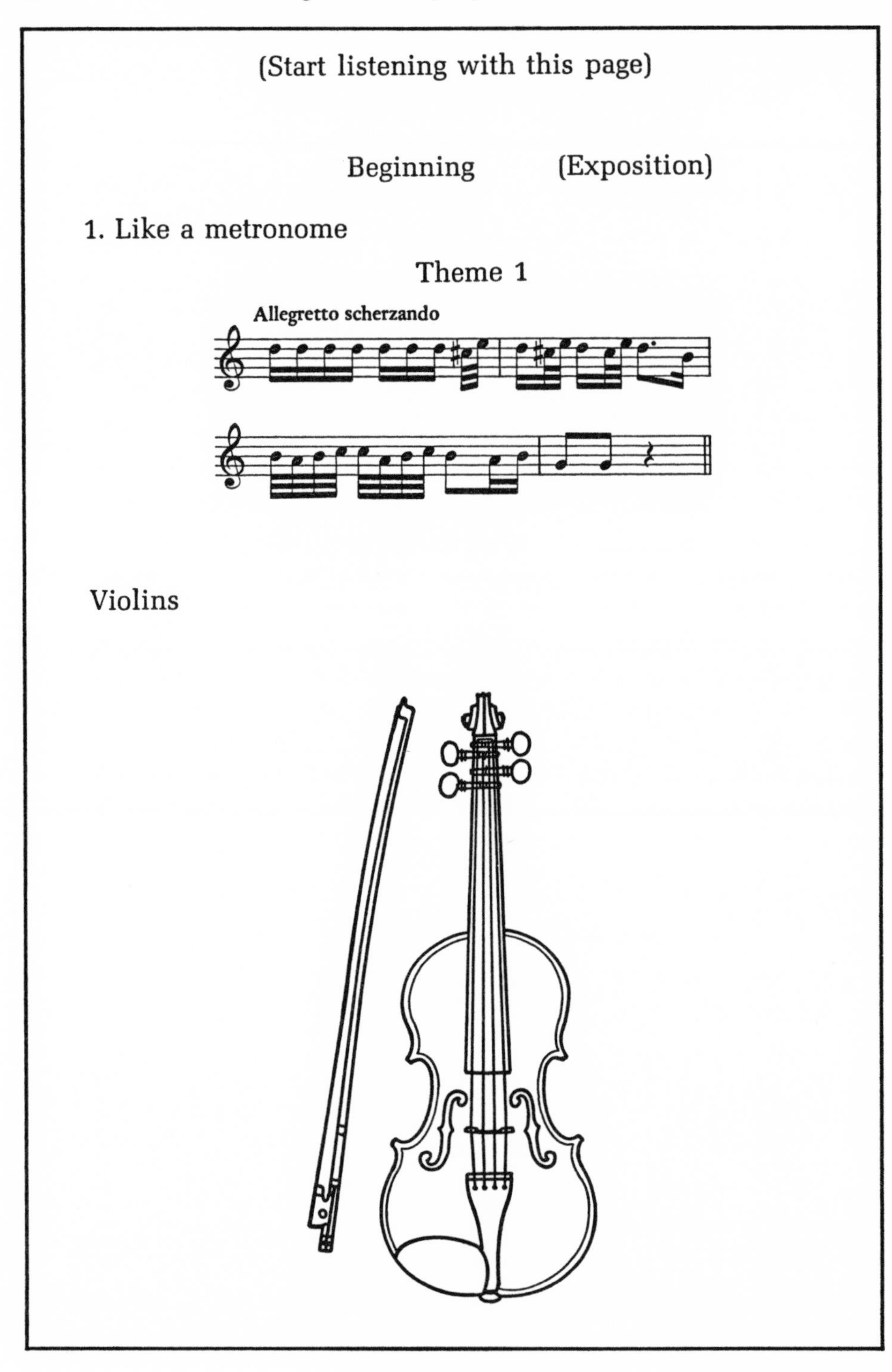
(Start listening with this page)
Beginning (Exposition)
1. Like a metronome
Theme 1
Allegretto scherzando
Violins

Figure 7-4

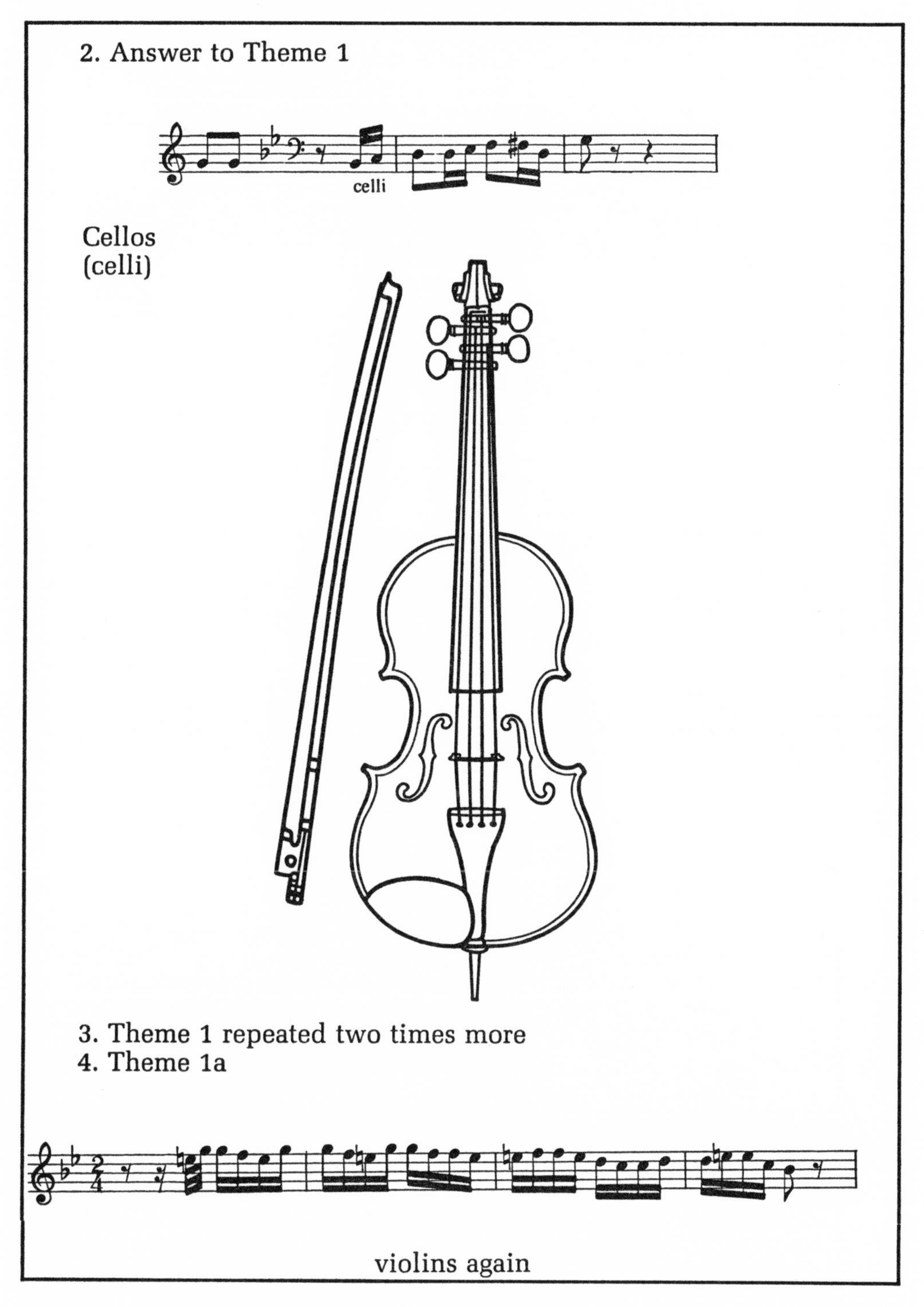
2. Answer to Theme 1
celli
Cellos
(celli)
3. Theme 1 repeated two times more
4. Theme 1a
violins again

Figure 7-5

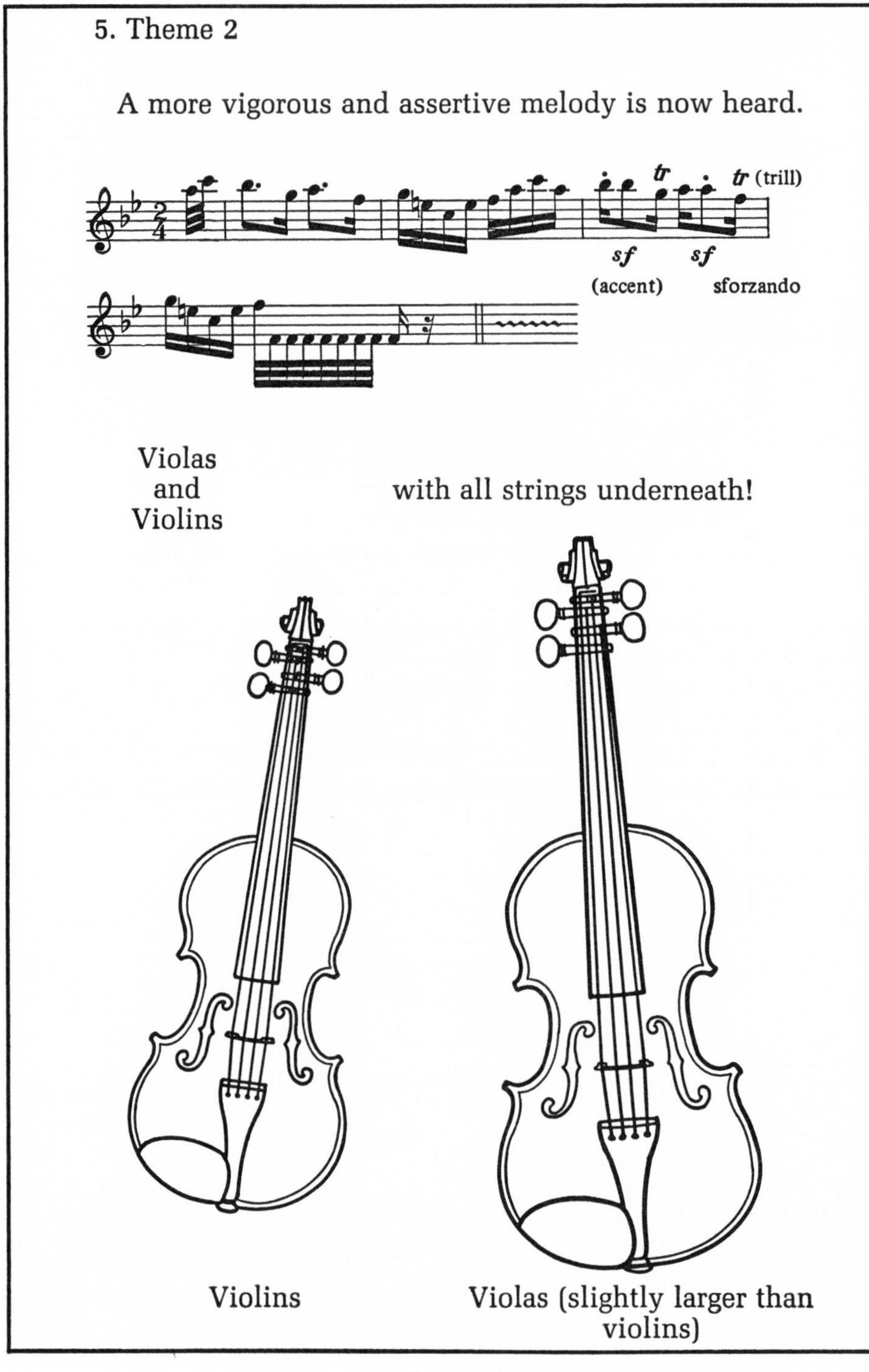
5. Theme 2
A more vigorous and assertive melody is now heard.
tr
tr (trill)
sf
sf
(accent)
sforzando
Violas
and
Violins
with all strings underneath!
Violins
Violas (slightly larger than violins)

Figure 7-6

6. Theme 3
(Repeated two times)
More mellow, smoothly flowing melody. Leads back to Theme 1.
It serves as a transition theme.
First played by woodwinds
Second time by strings

Figure 7-7

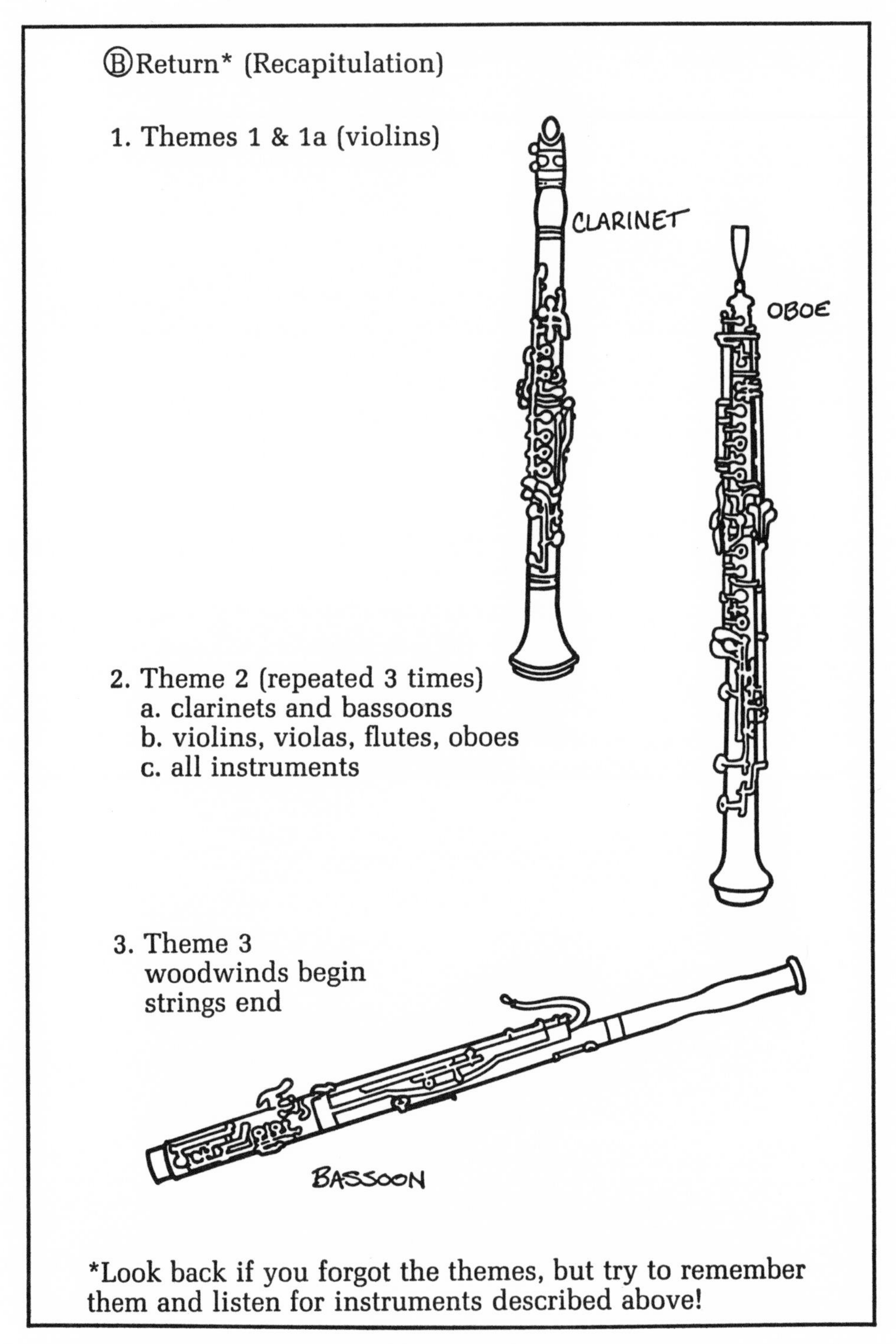

Ⓑ Return* (Recapitulation)

1. Themes 1 & 1a (violins)

2. Theme 2 (repeated 3 times)
   a. clarinets and bassoons
   b. violins, violas, flutes, oboes
   c. all instruments

3. Theme 3
   woodwinds begin
   strings end

*Look back if you forgot the themes, but try to remember them and listen for instruments described above!

Figure 7-8

ⒸCoda (Finale)
-ending-

1. Rhythmic figure

2. Answer

3. The above repeats to end in full orchestra.
Fortissimo (ff)

All Strings end with full orchestra.

Figure 7-9

3. Does it attract the students?
   a. Does it motivate?
   b. Does it stimulate?
4. Is it simple?
   a. Several ideas on one board is sometimes too complicated.
   b. Emphasize one or two ideas.
5. Is it easy to read?
   a. Is the lettering clear?
   b. Is the message easy to understand?

Things to Avoid in Bulletin Boards

A bulletin board should not be set up without careful planning. A presentation can easily become rambling and complex without a careful idea ahead of time. Sketch out the art work on a sheet of paper. Then do a trial layout on a table before you set it up permanently. Changes can then be made without damage to the individual parts.

Another consideration is to not keep the display up too long. A permanent type of bulletin board will become boring, unless it is changed frequently. College classrooms, in which different classes and teachers are using the same room, are often the most drab and unattractive rooms, because of a lack of bulletin board decorations. In school situations, where you will usually have fewer people using the same room, it, therefore, is easier to use the bulletin boards for display.

The bulletin board should not be too complicated. It shouldn't require so much preparation time that it becomes an infringement on regular lesson preparation. Also, don't always do it all yourself. Letting the students have a part in helping will increase interest.

If you always do the same type of bulletin board, the format will become routine and boring to the students and will not attract their attention as you would like. So, use variety.

SUMMARY OF TEACHING TECHNIQUES FOR GENERAL MUSIC

If you keep in mind a few definite concepts in all general music classes, your students will maintain a high level of interest and motivation. Conversely, a loose, disorganized class will result in a lack of interest, a poor attitude, and a less-than-serious feeling toward the course. Certain things that should be provided in your classes include the following:

1. Interesting subject matter
2. Information about the subject matter
3. Exploratory experiences in the subject
4. Development of desirable skills with the students
5. Opportunities for the students to discover the skills they may already have

The last two listed above can be put into effect by including the following activities that will acknowledge present skills and increase the students' development of other skills:

1. Provide analytical listening.
2. Provide for singing.
3. Provide for experience on instruments.
4. Provide practice in simple notation.
5. Relate music history to history and historical events.

Included in the above should be some long-term goals that you desire each student to accomplish:

1. Understand the place of music in society.
2. Develop attitudes to include music as a means of self-expression.
3. Develop the desire to continue in some type of music.
4. Develop a basis for evaluation of music (a realistic kind of evaluation).

CHAPTER 7 ENDNOTES

1. Glenn, Neal E., William B. McBride, and George H. Wilson. *Secondary School Music.* Englewood Cliffs, NJ: Prentice-Hall, 1970, 101.
2. Jacques-Dalcroze, Emile. *Rhythm, Music and Education.* London: Dalcroze Society, 1921.

Chapter 8

Electives That Can Be Taught with a Minimum of Preparation

Many high school music departments do not offer a system of music electives that can be used as enrichment or as required classes for a music major. Some schools teach the students music only through lessons and the major performing groups. Others offer music theory as the only high school classroom course. The reasons given for this lack of variety include not enough money, not enough staff, and problems in scheduling. In addition, the existing staff usually does not have enough time to prepare new electives.

Yet, as has already been discussed in Chapter 3, it is possible to schedule one-semester classes utilizing existing staff. This can be done without increasing expenditures by alternating years and electives. But how do you actually prepare and teach these electives? How do you find materials on the high school level? How much time does the preparation actually take? And can you do the necessary preparation within your already full schedule?

These problems and questions can be easily solved and answered in the affirmative. While published materials do tend to be utilized in the middle or elementary school, resources are available for high school use. And the preparation for these classes can be minimal.

ORGANIZING A SYSTEM OF ELECTIVES

In order to organize a system of electives, two main questions should be answered, the answers to which will largely determine the success rate of your program. While additional questions will surface also, the most important are:

1. What areas of elective possibilities interest me?
2. In what areas do I feel the students will be interested?

Before you order books, seek finances, and recruit students, the above questions should be answered and courses identified. If you try to teach a class just because you think it is important or possible but have no interest in that particular subject, you will probably find yourself teaching without any real enthusiasm. This, in turn, will lead to a lack of motivation in lessons and, thus, a lack of interest on the part of the students.

Also, if you offer courses that do not interest students, your recruiting efforts will be less than satisfactory. Sometimes, however, as discussed in Chapter 7, the name used in the course title can be a major factor in attracting students. Catchy titles are the way we seem to be indoctrinated by the media to respond. Books, records, television programs, and films tend to be more successful in attracting students when they have intriguing titles.

How can you organize good classes that will also interest students? First, you should survey the potential students. Distribute a form to all students, listing suggested course offerings and including a small description (see Figure 8-1). Ask the students to check those in which they would be interested. Leave a section for them to make

Student Elective Survey

The following courses may be offered next year as one-semester electives. Please check those that interest you the most. Number 1 will be your first choice, number 2 your second choice and so fourth.

At the bottom of the form is a section for your requests and interests.

Length	*Title*		*Credit*
1 semester	American Folk Music	_____	1/2
1 semester	Music of Modern America	_____	1/2
1 semester	European Music	_____	1/2
1 semester	American Musical Theater	_____	1/2
1 semester*	Song Writing	_____	1/2
1 semester	Electronic Music	_____	1/2

*Possible to extend this class for one full year.

Course Requests ________________________________

____

____

____

Student Name ____________________________ (optional)

Figure 8-1

suggestions as to their interests or to request electives. Finally, organize the following semester with those electives that have received the most positive responses.

Any other subjects that may be possible, or may be interesting to the students, could be added to the survey or replace those suggested. But once you have decided on courses to be offered, the next step would be to schedule them. The advantage of offering each class as a one-semester class is that you will be able to teach more electives in your program. A possible disadvantage might be a lack of time to go into depth. However, if classes meet five days per week for approximately twenty weeks, there should be time to teach a regular introductory-type class. Many college classes are set up on this basis.

In order to schedule electives, you will need to set up your program for at least two years (see Figure 8-2). A two-year plan should

Two-Year Plan (1 teacher)

Course	Year	Semester: Fall	Semester: Spring	Credit
Music Theory	1	X	X	1
Music Theater	2	X		½
American Folk Music	2		X	½
total credit				2

Two-Year Plan (2 teachers)

Course	Year	Semester: Fall	Semester: Spring	Credit
Music Theory	1	X	X	1
Modern American Music	1	X		½
Music Theater	1		X	½
Music History	2	X	X	1
Electronic Music	2	X		½
Folk Music	2		X	½
total credit				4

Figure 8-2

allow two teachers to handle the music courses. This will reduce expenditures, since you are using existing staff. Financing does not need to be a problem, since the only major needs will be textbooks and, possibly, recordings. Most schools have film libraries or access to them, which include many films on music and musicians. However, you may be in a situation where no available increases in finances are possible and you have no funds to implement the new courses. An alternative is the public library, which usually has free materials that can be used. Or, at least, this library is a member of a regional library system that has access to materials not at hand.

In Figure 8-2, a wide variety of classes is offered, each of which will require only one period per day per teacher. This is a very important consideration, since teacher time in the classroom is minimal. In addition, the maximum number of classes are taught.

PREPARING FOR ELECTIVES

Once your student survey is complete, and you have determined what courses should be offered, the next step will be to organize, and make a general outline of, the classes. This need not be time consuming. A very sketchy outline will help you identify those areas you may want to pursue in more detail. Figure 8-3 is an example of a preliminary course outline.

Each general period can be set up in the above simple outline. Following that, you may want a second column briefly describing the materials to use and some student work to be done, as in Figure 8-4.

In other words, from the outlines in Figures 8-3 and 8-4, you will get one very brief outline of where you are going and some idea of how you expect to achieve your goals. Student work and teacher expectations are also included. Each course can be set up in the above manner. Details can be filled in as you find materials, either before you begin the class or during it. The most important thing is that you have a plan and a method in which to execute it. Some suggested materials for music appreciation and history are:

Texts

McGehee, Thomasine C., and Alice D. Nelson. *People and Music.* Boston: Allyn and Bacon, 1973.

Music Appreciation and History

Baroque Period

I. Baroque Composers

A. Bach
B. Handel
C. Vivaldi
D. Purcell
E. Corelli
F. Couperin

II. Forms

A. Fugue
B. Concerto Grosso
C. Oratorio and Cantata
D. Opera

III. Concepts

A. Baroque Beginnings
B. Contrasts With Renaissance and Classical
C. Political Europe

IV. Religious and Secular Music

V. Instrumental and Vocal Music

Figure 8-3

Politoske, Daniel T. *Music*. Englewood Cliffs, NJ: Prentice-Hall, 1979.

Other Resource Texts

Hitchcock, H. Wiley. *Music in the United States: A Historical Introduction*. Englewood Cliffs, NJ: Prentice-Hall, 1969.

Method

I. Listening: Recordings

A. Student identification through listening tests
B. Some actual performances by students and faculty
C. Field trips to college concerts

II. Films

A. Library of composers' biographies
B. Filmstrip set—"History of Music"

III. Student Projects

A. Student reports—oral
1. composers
2. types of works
B. Questions answered as homework

Figure 8-4

Longyear, Rey M. *Nineteenth-Century Romanticism in Music.* Englewood Cliffs, NJ: Prentice-Hall, 1969.

Palisca, Claude V. *Baroque Music.* Englewood Cliffs, NJ: Prentice-Hall, 1968.

Filmstrips

The following filmstrips are coordinated with records for an audio-visual history of music:

1. "From the Beginnings Through the Middle Ages"
2. "High Renaissance"
3. "Age of the Baroque"
4. "Classical Age"
5. "Early Romanticism"

6. "Later Romanticism"
7. "Into the Twentieth Century"
8. "Music of Our Time"

These filmstrips are published by Educational Audio Visual, Inc., Pleasantville, NY 10570.

Here are some suggested music electives and descriptions:

Music Theory. This course traces the system of harmony as used during the "common practice period" from 1600 to c. 1820. Chords, melody writing, simple form, and orchestration will be included, along with ear training exercises to identify intervals and chord quality.

Music Appreciation and History. The general history of music and musical styles is discussed in order to help the student get a grasp of how music developed. All types of music will be looked at in order that the student might be able to discern different styles, concepts, and periods.

American Musical Theater. The unique style of music and drama known as the Broadway musical is taught from its beginnings to the present. The cultural and social mores of each period are discussed, along with the type of musical that was written during each time frame.

American Music and Modern America. In order to understand the cultural diversity and variety of music heard today, it is important to examine the unique way music was incorporated into our society from the time of the early colonists to the present day. Included in the examination will be the early New England Singing Schools, early attempts at public concerts, folk music of the plains, the west (i.e., the pioneers), and the rise of "popular music."

Song Writing. This course should be taken only after Music Theory is successfully completed. The focus will be on creativity. Beginning with simple phrases, the student will be taught to incorporate these into larger two- and three-part song forms. Harmonizations and rhythmic accompaniments will be encouraged so that students will be able to begin to express themselves musically.

Electronic Music. How a composer works in the electronic medium is the focus of this course. Making compositions through tape recorders and synthesizers is the aim of the class. In other words, the how-to approach will be taken. Works of successful electronic composers will be studied. Practical application is provided.

Folk Music. This course is concerned with a traditional oral art. It is the music of the people, the "folk"; thus, it follows the natural cultural history of these various peoples. How music was transmitted, improvised, composed, and so on are its focus.

HOW TO FINANCE AND STAFF ELECTIVES

As discussed in Chapter 3, a major increase in funds is not really necessary in order to initiate a system of electives. But just how do you take care of acquiring supplies and equipment? Many administrators are prone to say "no" to increases in programs because they fear the accompanying budget increase.

Yet new music classes can be taught without a major increase in funds. Various methods of implementing existing staff and resources include the following:

1. Staff teaches electives on an alternating semester or yearly basis.
2. Use handouts instead of textbooks. (This is not desirable, but possible if necessary.)
3. Use the library and individual research for additional materials instead of purchasing more supplies.

Chapter 9

How to Teach Unusual Music Classes: Contemporary, Electronic, Environmental, and Improvisational Music

The act of creating a music composition means, in a sense, experimenting with available sounds, rhythms, and timbres. The end result should be a piece of artistic worth. This is true even in the most rudimentary form of composition.

To understand the resources available to today's composers is to understand the experiment of music. It then becomes important for students to become acquainted with the various new musical idioms available for composers to use in their creative expressions. These may include contemporary, electronic, environmental, improvisational, chance music, and many others.

Often teachers are not as familiar with these types of compositional tools as they are with more traditional types of composition. But there are ways to teach these concepts without a great deal of research and expense.

HOW TO TEACH CONTEMPORARY MUSIC

Because much avant-garde music is new and different sounding, many of your students will not have much acquaintance with it. This may be especially true if the music has electronic and experimental (or chance) sounds in it. As a result, this new idiom may seem so strange to them that they will not perceive it as music. In addition, there is often an immediate tendency to dislike it.

You can lessen this tendency by preparing your students properly for what they are about to hear. First, explain the purposes of various avant-garde types of music. Why did composers seek a new method of expression? What did they try to accomplish and say in their music? Why are some still working with those new types of expression? Why aren't others?

In other words, explain the background of this music. Why doesn't it sound like "regular" music? Try to prepare students to hear sounds that will be totally new and different from anything else they may have heard before.

It is not very easy to teach an understanding and appreciation of this type of music, unless you also teach the cultural and political history of the era as it relates to composers' views of the world around them and the world of art. For instance, in the "new music" of 1900, the dissonant and serial forms were experimental, but they were related to the experiments of society. The shattering of most accepted political concepts in World War I caused composers to attempt to rebuild their culture, just as countries attempted to rebuild in the smoky rubble and devastation of Europe. New forms were sought because the old ones no longer existed.

Pitches were no longer considered to be separated by half steps. Instead, composers viewed pitch as a sort of constant within a continuum. It was an unbroken range of sound extending from the lowest to the highest pitches. The composer had the flexibility to be able to use any part of that continuum. This was a major development that found a place in much electronic music.

There was also a change in the known concepts of rhythm. Instead of regular deviation of pitches in set patterns, composers sought to use indeterminacy. In other words, there were no limits; these were left up to the performers. Only general instructions were given by the composer.

In addition, composers sought to use new sounds or timbres other than those generally available to them. For instance, instead of using only regular instruments, composers used new sounds, such as the "prepared" piano of Henry Cowell where strings were tuned differently. Oriental instruments were used. African instruments were used. Environmental instruments (those found in the natural environment) were used. Available mechanisms, such as tools, anvils, sirens, radios, and tape recorders (sometimes even with human voices recorded backwards) were also used.

When approaching serialism and the twelve-tone techniques, it is important to demonstrate why composers sought to work in these idioms. For instance, the twelve-tone concept of equality between tones should be studied. Freedom in harmony, another contemporary compositional technique, should be considered. This will help students understand unaccustomed tonalities. It is also important to study the freedom in thematic development and structure.

Remember, contemporary composers are attempting to say something in their music that reflects their belief in art, politics, or the world around them. Try to help the students to understand just what it is the composer is trying to say. Even such concepts as anti-art can be understood, if you emphasize the reasons why composers worked in this idiom. The acceptance of whatever happens for its own sake, with absolutely no control by anyone, creates a sense of anti-art. Intentional or unintentional sounds are included as part of the experience.

Equipment and Resources Needed for Units on Contemporary Music

Very little equipment is needed to teach contemporary musical trends. A phonograph, some recordings, and a tape recorder are basically it. The following methods can be used to experiment in contemporary idioms:

1. Experiment with existing instruments to produce new and unique timbres in nontraditional ways.
2. Search out other available objects to use as musical instruments.
3. Experiment with nontraditional notation in order for students to be free to create without the limitations of the staff notations.
4. Use a tape recorder to record, play back, and listen to experiments in music.
5. Let imaginations soar *unlimited* to any area of musical sounds that interest students without respect for traditional methods.

HOW TO USE ELECTRONIC MUSIC EFFECTIVELY

To learn electronic music, it is not necessary for students to have a background in music theory or any other musical training of a highly structured nature. Of course, the stronger the background, the greater the appreciation the student may have for new things, but this is not a requirement. The most important aspect of electronic music is to teach students how to use the equipment. That is, how can it be used to produce electronic sounds?

The basic tenet of electronic music will be that of a laboratory. The prime directives are to experiment and to create. The sound of created elements will direct the student towards his or her own goals.

An often-made mistake is that, in order to teach or work in the electronics medium, students and teachers should know a great deal about electronics. Yet this is not necessarily that important. Certainly, the more you know about the equipment and electronic circuitry, the more flexibility you have in utilizing the tools of the trade. Yet a lack of adequate electronic knowledge should in no way deter you from entering this field. In fact, if you know how to use a tape recorder, you can create in the electronic medium.

Many possible sounds can be made with a standard reel-to-reel recorder. And many of these sounds can be standard instruments or voices played back in an irregular manner. In fact, many famous compositions in the electronic medium simply are regular sounds played back in a different way. This *musique concrete* is just that. Developed during the 1950s, it consisted of taking musical sounds and environmental or nonmusical sounds and changing them in some sort of electronic manner, and then playing them back in a changed way.

Below are some things that students can do quite easily to produce electronically related music:

1. Record standard musical instruments on a multispeed tape recorder, and play back at a different speed.
2. Search out certain special effects for sounds that are unusual. These may include metal pipes, metal plates, or hollow containers.
3. Find environmental sounds such as wind, leaves rustling, running water, or sticks breaking.
4. Take any of the above and:
   a. Play back at a different speed.
   b. Reverse the tape so sounds will be heard backwards.

This list is just an example of what you can do to create unusual sounds that will be effective tools in the creation of electronic music. However, with the addition of two multispeed tape recorders, you can add more variety. For instance, you might do the following:

1. Record, with the sound of one tape recorder already made. Add new sounds on top of those and combine.
2. Combine standard sounds with "changed" sounds.
3. Combine forward sounds and reverse sounds.
4. Play the same sounds at one speed simultaneously with other sounds at another speed. Blend together.

The addition of more tape recorders gives you the ability to continue the above using a rich variety of manipulative sounds. Your imagination and that of your students will be the only limitations.

However, it is possible to utilize a highly complex system of electronic musical instruments, should you so desire and have the funds to do so. These might include the following:

amplifiers
loudspeakers
phonographs
electronic synthesizers
microphones
filters (to eliminate certain unwanted frequencies of sound)
modulators (which changes certain incoming sound waves)
reverberation-type units (to reverberate the sound produced)
mixer (to eliminate or add sounds to final product)

The complexities of some systems are astounding. Some studies have even more equipment, such as tape erasers, splicers, computer interfaces, and multihead tape recorders, etc. Depending on the amount of money you have to spend, the equipment is available. But, again, it really is not necessary to have such a complex system if you have limited funds or do not wish to invest so heavily.

Where to Find Electronic Music Information

Much informative material has been written about electronic music; some of it scholarly but a lot of it is practical in scope and is most useful in the high school situation. For those wishing to pursue the history of the medium, the following should be useful:

Cope, David. *New Directions in Music*. Dubuque, Ia: Wm. C. Brown Co., 1971.

Grout, Donald J. *History of Western Music*. New York: W. W. Norton, 1973.

Luening, Otto. "History of Electronic Music." *Music Educators Journal*, November 1968.

For the practical application of electronic techniques in the classroom, an excellent periodical is *Music and the Electronic Medium*, published by the State Education Department of New York. This book is loaded with resources for setting up a studio. Those wishing copies should write to the State Education Department in Albany, New York.

HOW TO ADD INTEREST THROUGH ENVIRONMENTAL MUSIC

Environmental music is really not new. From what we have read in history and studied in archaeology, ancient man used nature and natural sounds in his music. Indeed, even the American Indian continues to incorporate nature in his tribal songs and music. The sound of the wind, leaves, trees, water, animals, and birds is both listened to for its own sake and incorporated into man-made music.

Recently, composers have become interested in the possibilities of music created through the capturing of natural sounds found in the environment. Some sounds are used intact, others are changed electronically, some are synthetically copied. Most are stored by the use of the tape recorder. A whole new avenue of exploration is open to students where they are able to use their imaginations.

Equipment Needs and How to Use Them

The best way to begin with environmental sounds is through a tape recorder. This can be used in the classroom, or taken out and used to record sounds in nature. However, since our perception of the way things sound in nature is often directly connected with our senses, it is necessary to examine this closely. In other words, the sound of leaves rustling in the wind will be connected with your seeing the forest, feeling the temperature on your body, the wind to your back, and the feel of the ground beneath you. Yet an isolated sound put on a recorder may seem somehow different when not heard in context with the above. Therefore, our concept of certain sounds may turn out differently in reality. This is good to keep in mind, because it may add a different color to our recording.

It is also possible to produce synthetic sounds to imitate those in nature. This would be similar to the use of sound effects on radio programs. For instance, the sound of fire is often made by crinkling paper, bird sounds made by whistles, and so on. Therefore, it is possible to record "environmental" sounds without leaving the classroom.

Let your students use their imaginations while collecting these sounds. Once you get a large collection of different sounds, it becomes a simple chore of sequencing them as desired by recording them a second time on a second recorder in the order that the composer desires. As in electronic music, the sounds of stones, sticks, water, and wind can be changed by recording them at different speeds or playing them back in reverse. This will result in unusual "musical" sounds (environmental) being made even more unusual by electronic techniques. A truly unique sound of music can be sequenced.

Teaching Form through Environmental and Electronic Music

When using the symbols of environmental and electronic music, students will be working in a nontraditional idiom. Therefore, regular musical phrases, melodies, and rhythms will not be the same. But this type of music can still have form to it by establishing an overall balance in length, volume and rhythmic sequences. In other words, students should be encouraged to have their compositions balanced with some thought to the general structure and final impression that the work may have regarding a form.

In fact, students will most likely learn the intrinsic concepts of form and structure simply by experimentation. They can also work to establish variety in their works, as well as a general length that "fits" the style of the created work. This, in turn, should carry over to the more traditional styles of composition, which will have metrical forms established within the staff.

HOW TO TEACH IMPROVISATION IN THE CLASSROOM

It has been widely recognized that much of the art of improvisation, which was so popular in earlier days, has been lost. Bach, as well as others, used to improvise entire fugues on a given theme. Most cadenzas in concertos were never written out. Composers, instead, left it up to the individual performers to improvise a cadenza. In fact, in many concerts there was a time set for improvised music by a soloist.

Today, with the exception of the stage band and other jazz ensembles, most performers do not improvise at all. Actually most players, students and professionals, become very inhibited if required to do any extemporaneous-type playing without written notes. Along with this, the concept of realizing the figured bass has become a lost technique.

Figured bass was a musical shorthand used, particularly, in the Baroque period. Composers would write the bass line only, with numbers put in from time to time designating chords to be added by the player when performing the work. Only the general outline was written in the figured bass. The actual chords and placement of notes were to be put in by the performer in the general style of the composition. Since this was a fairly loose system each player would "realize" the figured bass in a slightly different way, and improvise the harmony. As this was the accepted method to perform most accompaniment-type keyboard pieces, performers were most

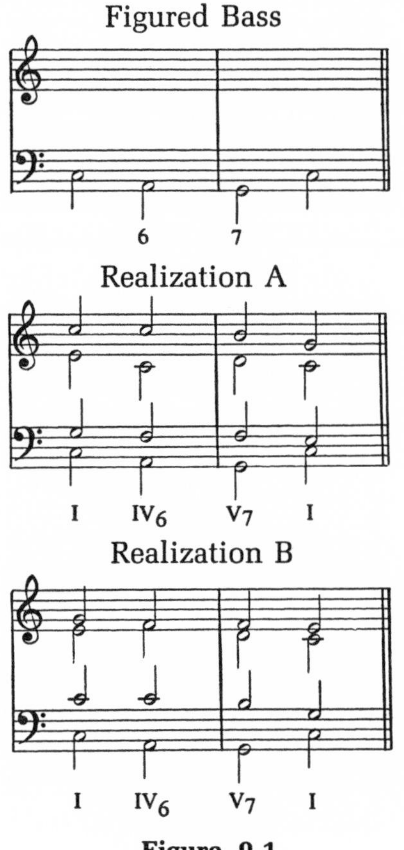

Figure 9-1.

proficient in at least this aspect of improvisation (see Figure 9-1).

Given the opportunity, however, most students can quickly learn how to improvise a part or even a whole composition. But the problem has been that they seldom get the opportunity to try. We have often become too structured. In fact, Emile Jacques-Dalcroze in his book, *Rhythm, Music and Education,*[1] wrote a chapter called, "Rhythmic Movement, Solfege and Improvisation." This chapter is a proponent for rhythmic movement (physical movement) being the nearest element of music to life. This system of rhythmic physical exercises, called eurythmics, aims to strengthen the power of concentration. He includes a series of physical movements that, if done, will enable the student to "invent" free movements that can be translated to musical tones.

The following is an example of improvised movements:

1. Set a basic rhythmic beat.
   a. Move right and left arms in circular motions.
   b. Reverse motions.
   c. Enlarge or make smaller motions.
   d. Move upper torso in circular motions.
   e. Reverse motions.
   f. Enlarge or make smaller.
2. At a specific rhythmic beat, but different from 1, have students "improvise" the above movements.

There is a basic general feeling that this improvised physical movement will carry over to improvised tones. Reasons for this are that the nerve synapses can become conditioned for extemporaneous movement, which will help in transposing this spontaneous thinking into music.

When beginning transpositions in musical lines, the students should start with what they know. The two easiest methods are scales and chords. First, start with scales being played in rhythmic variations. Second, have the students skip various notes. Third, incorporate arpeggios in the I-IV-V-I sequence, and proceed to other chords as they become familiar. In this way, students will be familiar with scales and chords in various keys and will be able to begin a systematic approach to general improvised music.

Once the above elements have been learned, the next step is to pick a specific style of music and play the improvised techniques in that type of style. It does not have to be jazz or classical. You can use any style of music that students are familiar with and proceed with scales, arpeggios, and skipped notes in that idiom.

The next step in the technique of improvisation is to begin incorporating the techniques into actual melodies of freely improvised samples. It does not matter how simple they may be. Students will gradually learn to improvise and elaborate them. Also, try not to let your students become self-conscious as to whether or not the melodies sound good or have mistakes. Play whatever comes out and learn from it. Improvised playing is a learning experience, and mistakes are part of the process.

Continuing this program, from the simple to the complex, will enable the students to improvise freely. It will not happen overnight, but gradually all students can learn to improvise, the advantages of which are:

1. increased awareness of melodic elements (melody, harmony, and rhythm)
2. increased technical facility
3. tone control (dynamics and sound)

CHAPTER 9 ENDNOTES

1. Jacques-Dalcroze, Emile. *Rhythm, Music and Education.* London: Dalcroze Society, 1921.

Chapter 10

How to Keep Accurate Records

Records! Accurate Records! Too often these are considered to be too much trouble. We all know they are important, but there is just too much to do to keep up with all the other aspects of the music program. Common complaints may be: "There just isn't enough time to do the regular teaching, let alone keep written records." There is very little free time in my schedule." "The school has put too many other nonmusical duties in my schedule, so I do not have office time." "I can remember the important things anyway; why write them down?"

There are answers to all the above excuses for not keeping accurate records, except perhaps the last one. The person who is blessed with an unfailing memory is blessed indeed. For the rest of us mortals, however, written notes can help greatly in the mental recall of important things.

Keeping records need not entail an efficient office staff nor does it have to include complicated filing systems. A simple record system can be set up so that, once it is organized, it will free the teacher for important teaching time and will require minimal effort and time to update.

WHY RECORDS ARE NECESSARY

If students are to progress systematically, they will need to accomplish certain levels of playing and singing. In order to achieve these levels, they will need method books and etudes or songs, and will need to learn solos and perform in organizations. It is difficult to remember which student is in what situation, or what each has accomplished. When a student moves and a letter of recommendation is requested, then it becomes your responsibility to record accurately the student's progress so that the new teacher will know where the student is musically. These types of records are done judiciously in the academic and social areas of a student's school life, but very little is done on the musical side.

In addition, students often take music classes and private study, and perform outside the school situation. These are all part of the student's musical education and should be included as accomplishments in the records of each student.

HOW RECORDS OF VARIOUS TYPES CAN SIMPLIFY YOUR JOB

Records can be kept on simple forms that will require one or two words and are accurate and easily done. For instance, an instrumental student's accomplishments can be recorded from the time the student begins the instrument, and can continue throughout his or her high school career. This record is a *positive* listing (see Figure 10-1). The purpose is not to point out problems, but rather to record the accomplishments of each student.

Some other types of simple record cards that are very handy to have available might include music sign-out sheets and instrument assignment sheets. Most music teachers, who have students on a pri-

Student Accomplishments

Development and Performance Record

Name ________		*Solos*	*Year*
Instrument ________		________	____
Other Instruments ________		________	____
	Year		
Method Books ________	____		
________	____		
________	____		
________	____	*Festivals*	
________	____	(County, etc.)	*Year*
________	____	________	____
________	____	________	____
Technique:			
Scales ________	____	________	____
Arpeggios ________	____	________	____
Tone ________	____	________	____
Musicianship ________	____	________	____

Remarks: ________

Figure 10-1

Instrument Inventory

Instrument ______________ Serial No. ______________
Make ______________ Cost ______________
Purchased ______________

Remarks: ______________________________
____

Name	Year	Out	In
1.			
2.			
3.			
4.			
etc.			

Figure 10-2

vate basis, are familiar with one age-old problem—lost personal music. Students do not always have the exact music that you wish them to play at a given time. Therefore, the simplest thing to do is to let them "borrow" one of your copies. Over a period of time most of us forget who has what or where; and the result is the same—lost music. With the large number of public school instrumental students in a program, the problem of misplaced music is compounded. The same can happen when school instruments are assigned to a student.

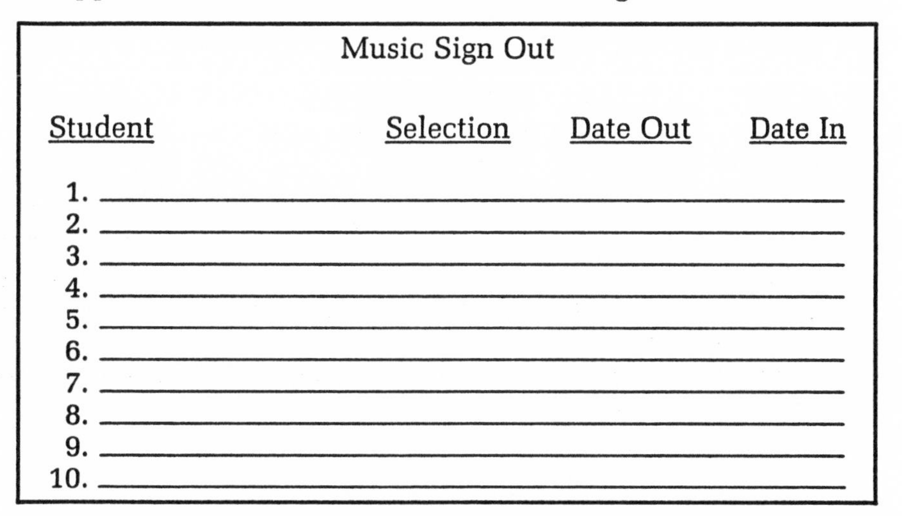

Music Sign Out

Student	Selection	Date Out	Date In
1.			
2.			
3.			
4.			
5.			
6.			
7.			
8.			
9.			
10.			

Figure 10-3

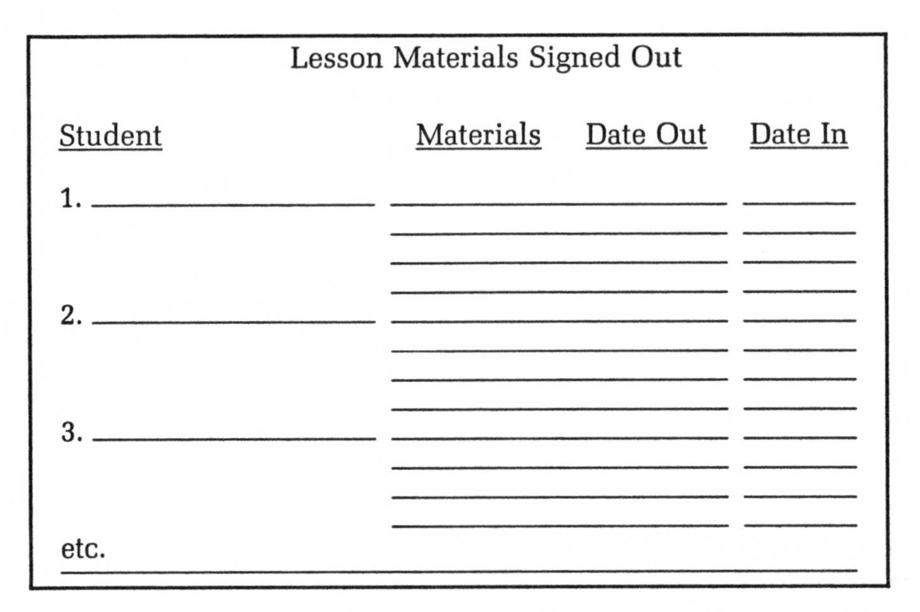
Lesson Materials Signed Out

Student	Materials	Date Out	Date In
1. ______			
2. ______			
3. ______			
etc.			

Figure 10-4

The problem can easily be solved through simple forms of inventory control (see Figures 10-2 through 10-4). Method books, solos, and ensemble music as well as instruments can be accounted for, and the forms only take a few seconds to complete. Remember, these are designed for *minimum* office work. You can be as complex as you wish, but these forms are efficient and quick to complete!

SMALL ENSEMBLES AND RECORD KEEPING

Students from time to time often desire to be assigned to a small ensemble. While the main student accomplishment card can record most of the musician's endeavors, a separate ensemble record is helpful in seeing that the student progresses in his or her ensemble experience and does not stagnate. Again, do not rely on your memory to know just what organizations the student was a member of and completed successfully. Rather, jot down a note or two as to which ensemble experience he or she has completed.

One result of keeping accurate records is that they will show when the student is ready for ensemble participation. When you have several students on one type of instrument, sometimes it becomes difficult to choose who should play in which ensemble. Records will point out certain clues that should help you in your decision. For example, one horn player you teach might have developed a large, robust, brassy tone, while another has developed a small articulate sound. If this is so recorded, you might note that the student who developed a robust tone might fit in a brass quintet nicely while the small sound would, perhaps, be just right for a woodwind quartet.

In addition, by recording the general musicianship of the students as well as the technique learned, you can better determine which ensemble and which level or advancement would work best for each player or vocalist. Don't try to be complicated. Just record the facts (see Figure 10-5).

Ensemble Recommendation Card

Name ____________________
Year ____________________

Ability		Interest		
General	______	Brass	______	___
Blending	______	Woodwind	______	___
		Mixed		
Qualities	______	Ensembles	______	___
Tone	______			
Experience	______	Recommendation		1. ___
				2. ___

Figure 10-5.

STORAGE OF INSTRUMENTS AND INVENTORIES

While storing unused musical instruments is basically a matter of keeping them on the shelf, it is a little more complicated to keep accurate inventories of the same (see Figure 10-6). Information that is useful for each instrument includes the following:

1. make and serial number
2. purchase price

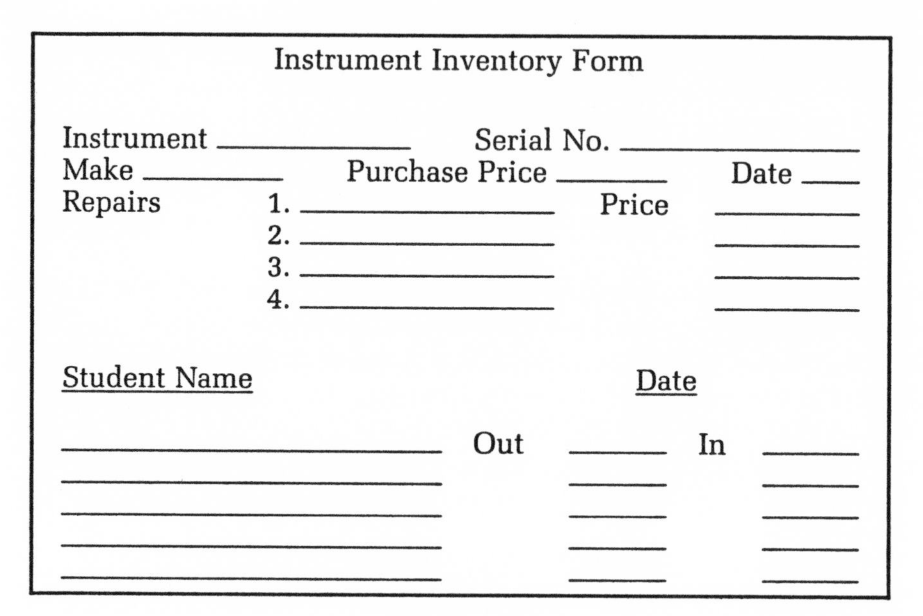

Instrument Inventory Form

Instrument ______ Serial No. ______
Make ______ Purchase Price ______ Date ______
Repairs 1. ______ Price ______
2. ______ ______
3. ______ ______
4. ______ ______

Student Name — Date

______ Out ______ In ______
______ ______ ______
______ ______ ______
______ ______ ______
______ ______ ______

Figure 10-6

3. age
4. repairs (when, what for, how much?)
5. active report—who played it?
6. inactive report—not used? For how long?

From Figure 10-6, you can quickly tell if the instrument is regularly used or not. If an instrument is constantly in use but is showing a lot of wear, it may be time to think about replacing it. A quick glance at your inventory sheet will tell you this.

Another important thing an inventory list should tell you is the instrument's depreciation. After an instrument is purchased, it begins to depreciate. At a certain point it will actually have no practical resale value. This is the time (if not before) to replace it with a new or good used horn. This is the only way you will be able to maintain value in the equipment.

HOW TO SIMPLIFY REPORTING TO PARENTS

In most school districts some sort of report card is sent home with the students, indicating their general level of academic standing. Grades used are usually numerical or by letter. In some cases only two letters are used as a general indication of the student's progress: *S* (satisfactory) and *U* (unsatisfactory). Whether by letter or number, there seems to be a deficiency in this system of reporting when applied to music. This system is designed for academic accountability, the percent of right answers, or material versus the wrong amounts. For example, a grade of eighty-seven would indicate 87 percent correct, 13 percent wrong.

However, the above does not indicate the creative aspect. In other words, how do you measure the student's progress in relation to his or her inherent talents? This is not indicated by a grade. In addition, musical progress cannot always be measured by numbers. True, one can actually count the number of "wrong notes" in an exercise and come up with a numerical grade. But how do you account for musical interpretation, musicianship, stage presence (if applicable), or attitude?

To solve the above dilemma, it might be useful to send home a student progress report that is more detailed and informative than a grade. Parents can tell just how well their child is doing in his or her musical studies. In addition, it will become clear if any marked deficiencies need attention.

Refer to Figure 2-1 in Chapter 2 for a sample student evaluation form to be sent to parents.

Chapter 11

How to Simplify Fund Raising

Music departments need money! Some are fortunate to be in districts that are affluent and receive large music budgets. Many, however, are in average income communities that are hard pressed to keep operating expenses flowing into the schools.

Yet instruments, music, and supplies, like most other things, are expensive and constantly rising in price. Financing the needs of a music department becomes more and more difficult. Schools can pay for only so many new instruments. However, a growing productive band or orchestra will need better-quality instruments, as the organization matures. Choral music is expensive. One selection will require a large amount of money to buy a copy for each student.

As a result, many music organizations feel the need to have fund-raising activities. Sometimes this can result in a large amount of working funds for the organization. Sometimes, however, it can lead to an added burden to an already crowded teaching schedule. Unfortunately, some fund-raising activities can also result in a lack of success, with very little profit to show for the efforts.

Fund raising should be successful, smooth, profitable, simple, and as brief as possible. Anything else can result in unwanted complications. The purpose of this chapter is to show you how to succeed in fund raising.

THE ESSENTIALS OF FUND-RAISING TECHNIQUES

In order to have a smooth operation that can generate the most profits, take the least amount of time, require the least amount of paperwork on your part, and have the most community support, some essentials should be adhered to completely. Without considering these, you may not have a trouble-free campaign. With all of these taken into consideration, you can minimize problems that may arise during the allotted time.

These essentials will include the following:

1. coordination with other fund-raising groups within the school
2. coordination with other fund-raising groups within the community

3. advance publicity to the community including:
   a. who—group
   b. why—purpose of funds
   c. when—exact dates
4. Appointed committees within the group to take care of paper work, check on students, and count and deposit money
5. complete understanding as to the help that can be expected from the company salesman

HOW TO COORDINATE FUND RAISING WITHIN THE SCHOOL

Some very difficult problems in a fund-raising campaign can occur when groups within a school do not coordinate their activities. The results can be a duplication of efforts and fewer profits for all. If organizations do not cooperate, it is possible to have two or more groups selling the same type of product with many of the same students in both organizations.

If too many people constantly ask members of the community for support, it may begin to wear thin. This may be especially true in small communities where the same people have students knocking on their doors for everything.

The best way around this dilemma is to have a general in-school fund-raising calendar on which all organizations will coordinate their campaigns (see Figure 11-1). Each group signs up for a time schedule with maximum allowable campaigns per session.

If your school does not use the above, it would be good for you to suggest that it be initiated. A lot of selling confusion can be eliminated when everyone knows what is going on in the whole school.

COORDINATING WITH OTHER FUND-RAISING GROUPS IN THE COMMUNITY

Coordinating fund-raising activities with other groups in the community is sometimes difficult, as there is usually no central area to go to in order to schedule events on a unified calendar. As a result, it may be almost impossible to try to schedule nonconflicting activities. However, you can try calling a few of the organizations in town.

School Fund-Raising Coordinating Calendar

October 19xx

Sunday	Monday	Tuesday	Wednesday	Thursday	Friday	Saturday
				1	2	3
4	5 Candle Sale	6	7 Home Ec Club	8	9	10
11	12 Candy Sale	13	14 Senior Band	15	16	17
18	19 Poster Sale	20	21 10th Grade Class	22	23 Magazine	24
25	26 Sale	27 Senior Class	28	29 Record Sale	30	31 Senior Chorus

Figure 11-1

Or you may ask one of your officers to call, thus alleviating the necessity of your doing it all.

Even a minor attempt at coordination is better than not trying at all. You may be able to eliminate a problem, and it will most certainly improve your commmunity relations.

SENDING ADVANCE PUBLICITY TO THE COMMUNITY

A successful fund-raising activity needs to have community support. This support will come more easily if people know some things about the event. Simply put, this means the basics: who, what, when, where, and why. Inform them of these basics and they will be more likely to help you in the campaign. You can start by making posters, explaining that the coming fund-raising activity is raising money for a specific purpose—uniforms, a trip, new instruments, or another necessary item. In addition, the people like to know the ways in which their contributions will be used.

It is also important to let everyone know just how long the event will last. If the campaign is to last one week, make sure your students do not knock on doors after the scheduled closing date. You can wear out your welcome rather quickly once you go past the last scheduled date of the sale!

How to Keep the Community Interested in Your Group's Efforts

You will want and need the support of your townspeople and you don't want to make them disturbed by your efforts. In order to keep public relations on a high level of friendliness, there are some basic points to follow:

1. Announce ahead of time when the campaign is to begin.
2. State the purpose of the funds to be earned.
3. Give ending dates. Stop on time!
4. Coordinate your salespeople so they will not duplicate efforts with customers. In other words, don't let more than one salesperson call upon a customer.

5. Let customers know exactly whom to call in case of a problem with the salesperson, product, or other difficulty. You should supply them with:
   a. salesperson in the group to contact
   b. company complaint number
   c. company address

Expressing Appreciation to the Community

Once you have completed your fund-raising activities, and the aforementioned items have been dealt with, it will be appropriate to express your appreciation to the community for their support. This is an excellent way to ensure their continued support for future events. And when you do this, remember that there are some simple items to include:

1. whether or not you reached your goal
2. what you purchased with the funds
3. how much you appreciate all the support from the community

There are various methods for reaching the community with your expressed appreciation.

1. Put a notice in the local paper, even if you have to pay for it.
2. Put a thank-you notice in the school newsletter or newspaper.
3. Put posters around town in conspicuous places.
4. Send announcements by way of local radio stations.

APPOINTING COMMITTEES TO KEEP RECORDS

In any fund-raising event, a certain amount of paper work needs to be done. While this can be time consuming, it should not, however, take up any more than a minimal amount of your time. You will remove most potential headaches if you delegate responsibilities to committees.

The following two committees should be formed:

1. coordinating committee
2. treasury committee

The Coordinating Committee

The purpose of the coordinating committee is to keep track of each student's progress during the campaign. This includes such things as noting the number of items each student has taken, making sure each student turns in extra or leftover items, keeping track of supplies (i.e., sales items) needed during the length of the event, and general record keeping.

Keep this committee as small as possible in order to keep it efficient. If your group is divided into teams, then each one can use the team captain as the committee leader. Remember that the purpose of the committee is to relieve you of extra time-consuming book work.

The Treasury Committee

The treasury committee will be responsible for collecting, recording, counting, and depositing the money. Often this is the most complicated part of the campaign. But if you allow the committee full responsibility for handling (providing they are competent to do so) all the counting (or another job) of the money, it will be a great burden relieved from your shoulders.

The group treasurer should be the committee chairperson. Under this person will be those members whose primary responsibility will be to collect and count the money. The treasurer's job will be to record and deposit it.

Following these simple and basic rules will make your job easier and will help the campaign operate smoothly; however, failure to adhere to these procedures could cause much frustration and work on your part.

WHAT YOU CAN EXPECT FROM THE COMPANY SALESPERSON

Many fund-raising problems can be eliminated, if you know that you can rely on reasonable help from the salesperson or company representative. These problems can deal with many areas: leftover sales products, incorrect billing and percentage of profits, damaged items, or customer complaints relating to the product. In addition, one frustrating thing can occur when the sales representative does not appear to be easily available for answering questions.

Before you go into a fund-raising activity, be sure you know what you can expect in the way of help from the company. After having gone through many campaigns with various companies, I have found that this help can vary. Below are the two most common ways that companies deal with schools:

1. The company ships the products—salesperson arrives shortly to help with distribution—salesperson checks regularly during the sale by phone or in person to see how things are going—salesperson returns at end of campaign to help wrap it up.
2. Salesperson makes big pitch to get your business—company ships products—the rest is *up to you!*

The second of the above methods is not at all uncommon. Therefore, unless you are ready to solve all unforeseen problems that may come up during the length of the fund-raising activity, you should specifically ask for additional help and expect to know when the salesperson will return, where he or she can be reached in a hurry, and how much help can be expected in tying up loose ends at the end of the campaign.

I have actually had a salesperson write up the contract, and then never hear from him again. This has happened more than once. When problems arose, there was only one thing to do—solve them myself. As a result, I always check carefully before doing business with any company. It is important to know just how far the company is willing to go in offering help during the campaign.

Don't just expect their help. Ask in advance what they will do, how often they will come, and what they will do at the end of the campaign. It can eliminate a lot of headaches.

TECHNIQUES FOR A QUICK FUND RAISER

An important point to remember in any fund-raising technique is that the longer the campaign takes, the slower the sales tend to take place and the greater will be the lack of interest on the part of the students. It is, therefore, important when you set up your campaign that you schedule *exact* dates.

A second point to remember is to stick to those dates exclusively! Once the campaign has officially ended, the students must stop selling immediately. There are some very good reasons for stopping on schedule. First, it will encourage the students to start fund raising early in the campaign and not to wait until the last moment. Also, as stated earlier, it is better for your public relations if the community knows that the campaign will take place only between certain dates. It is like Halloween. Most community residents will give in and have their evening disrupted by little "demons" when they know it takes place only once. Spread this out over several nights, and patience might begin to wear thin.

KEEPING STUDENTS MOTIVATED DURING A LONG FUND RAISER

Sometimes it may be necessary or advantageous to extend the length of a fund raiser. This may include certain factors such as a school vacation, schools being closed due to bad weather, student illnesses, or perhaps a delay in delivering the products to be sold. Also, the type of sale might lend itself to a longer campaign. Magazine and record sales are often two or more weeks long, because customers usually like to keep the catalogs and look through them first for a few days before deciding on an order.

The problem of a longer time limit is largely one of trying to keep motivation up. Students may tend to let things ride during the middle of the event, and make a special effort only at the beginning and the end of the campaign. This defeats the purpose of the length of the fund-raising effort. Therefore, you should attempt some things that will encourage the students to continue their best efforts.

One thing that you can do in this area is to have some surprise additional prizes to give out. Usually a fund raiser begins with the annoucement of prizes for the highest and second-highest salespersons. Other prizes include certain things for those who have sold up to a certain level. However, by including additional prizes, heretofore unknown, you can keep motivation high throughout the campaign. Here are some effective methods:

1. Bring out a special prize on a Friday, and announce that it will go to the person who has sold the most over the week-

end. This does not affect other prize goals, but is separate from regular prizes.

2. Have several prizes that you can announce in the lull of the campaign. "Anyone who sells $50.00 or more in two days gets one of these!"
3. In addition to the highest winner, you might announce: "Anyone who sells $300.00 worth or more automatically gets this prize, even if you aren't the highest winner." This will encourage high sellers to keep their pace up, even if they know they can't catch up to the highest.

THE LONG-TERM GOALS OF FUND RAISING

Fund-raising events, even the longer ones, can be relatively easy to operate and motivate. Even a two-week event is not long to keep some sort of motivation going. The problem, then, that can develop in attempting to raise funds, is that you have a long-term goal requiring several events before the financial goals are achieved. Students easily lose sight of a long-term goal. One year may seem very short to us, but it often seems endless to high school students. A goal to be met in April will seem an eternity away in September. Also, there will often be a down time during the middle of the year, as students have trouble realizing the final efforts are in sight. They will often view another fund-raising event as just one more in a never-ending series.

There are, however, several things you can do to help keep student interest high. At the outset of the campaign, carefully explain the purpose of the total effort. What is the purpose of the money? If it is a lengthy campaign, then the goals must be important enough to keep the interest of the students. Some sample goals are:

1. band uniforms
2. concert piano
3. group trip

In other words, make sure that the result of your efforts is sufficient to encourage the students to do their best. Just to say we need money for music, supplies, or instruments is not enough. What instruments? Be specific. Music for a special concert? What music? Students need to know the results of their efforts. And the results should be sufficient to warrant their extra-long efforts.

Chapter 12

Financing Music Department Needs on an Economical Budget

Like everything else, music and supplies have greatly increased in price. In fact, less than half of the usual department needs can be financed by a budget that just a few years ago seemed adequate. Unfortunately, with community tax awareness groups and others becoming increasingly influential, school boards are very reluctant to add funds to present budgets. Yet each year departmental budgets will purchase less and less.

The preceding circumstances present a very real problem: trying to maintain present levels of departmental needs without considering increases in supplies. A common complaint among many school districts is that departments are losing ground by simply trying to maintain the status quo. Still, funds become more difficult to obtain each year.

As a result, it is most important that music departments organize an accurate budget, estimate needs correctly and positively, and impress their needs on the administration. Indeed, convincing them may be your most important consideration.

THE IMPORTANCE OF ACCURATE BUDGETING

Credibility! This one word may become paramount in your attempt to figure annual music budgets. Music teachers often have an idea of how much money they need. Expressing this need in terms of exact figures is very important. Budget needs should be figured in a businesslike manner, with an estimate that will clearly show all the various monetary expenditures expected for the following year. It is certainly not enough to guess at a round figure and expect business departments to give credence to your requests. You need a complete breakdown in the categories for which you expect to spend funds.

In other words, you will need to set up a zero-based budgeting operation. For example, if you had $3,000 last year, it cannot be expected that you will automatically get at least that much again. Instead, you must start from zero and account for your dollar expenditures until you feel you have estimated your needs accurately.

In this way, you are adding credibility to your requests. Administrations will be more apt to view your budget estimates seriously when they feel you are not simply guessing. If you do not receive your funds in their entirety, at least administrators will not be likely to cut your budget arbitrarily. They will need to see where funds can be cut and still have functioning departments.

HOW TO DIVIDE THE MUSIC BUDGET ACCURATELY

After you have arrived at a budget, it will be necessary to divide your budget into separate categories. Each category should be specific as to the needs and the monetary figures.

Music

First, let's start with the music library. If you are budgeting for chorus, band, or orchestra, you might want to set up a systematic procedure for buying various types of music. A certain percentage will be set up for concert arrangements, marches, ensembles, and solos. If your annual budget is $1,000, you might want to organize it in the following manner:

concert music	60 percent	$ 600
marches and light music	20 percent	200
ensembles	15 percent	150
solos	5 percent	50
		$1,000

In the above manner, you will have set for yourself a control mechanism that will enable you to have a positive growth in the quality of your acquisitions. A word of caution: Be careful that you do not buy too much of the "latest hit" type music in the popular field. The reason for this is that usually after one or two years the music will be passe´ and your library will contain several expensive scores that will be rarely, if ever, done again. The temptation to purchase these popular tunes will be great *momentarily*. But it may be better to buy more music that will contain lasting "replay" value for your groups.

Equipment

Under the category "Equipment" will come such items as music room furnishings, instruments, and audio visual materials (i.e., sound systems, phonograph systems, and so on). Some schools are fortunate in that room furnishings are financed outside the music budget and come under general school supplies or maintenance. Others have a separate audio visual department, which supplies the needs of all the school's electronic component systems. However, if all the above supplies come out of your budget, you should make an attempt to supply a priority list when you submit your final budget.

If you can get by with one less filing cabinet, it may be better to purchase your music or that needed clarinet and get by with stacking your supplies for one more year. Setting priorities, in other words, is a very important aspect in your planning. We all do this in our personal lives, because there is only so much money to go around and some things are more important than others.

Therefore, set up your equipment purchases as priority items. For instance, suppose your equipment budget is $2,000. Your needs include two clarinets, a tenor saxophone, a flute, two filing cabinets, a new speaker for your sound system, and shelves for a second bookcase in the music room. Projected prices for these items are as follows:

2 clarinets @ $240	$ 480
1 flute	240
1 tenor sax	550
2 filing cabinets @ $250	500
speaker	500
shelves	80
	$2,350

With a cost overrun of $350, you are obviously going to cut something. But rather than arbitrarily reducing the budget, do it by comparing prices now and in the future. Perhaps it is not best to purchase the instruments first and other things later. In some cases, musical instruments have had fairly steady prices in the last few years, while some other items have increased more.

	This Year	Projected Price Next Year	
2 clarinets	$ 480	$ 520	
1 flute	240	260	
1 tenor sax	550	550	
TOTAL	$1,270	$1,330	(increase of $60)

2 filing cabinets	550	600	
speaker	500	650	
shelves (lumber)	80	120	
TOTAL	$1,080	$1,370	(increase of $290)

In the above illustration, the cost of delaying the purchasing of instruments or other equipment will differ. It may be best to purchase the equipment now and save the projected increase. Instruments could be purchased next year without a large increase in funds.

increase in supplies	$290
increase in instruments	$ 60
possible savings	$230

The above are only estimates. You should investigate what the projected estimates for price increases will be for the next fiscal year.

HOW TO CALCULATE EQUIPMENT DEPRECIATION

Musical instruments, like any other new purchase, have a depreciation rate that decreases the resale value as well as the inventory value of those items purchased. The longer you have a certain group of instruments, the lower your calculated instrument value will be. Eventually, you would reach a theoretical point where your inventory would have zero dollar value. As a result, you should have a program to upgrade and replace older instruments.

How do you calculate instrument depreciation? Insurance companies may suggest various ways but, as a rule, there is a simple way to get a "ball-park" estimate. You may depreciate approximately 20 percent per year of each year's estimated worth. Below is a suggested table:

Depreciation Table

Conn Cornet	Purchase Price	$240.00
Depreciation Record:	Year 1	192.00
	2	153.60
	3	122.88
	4	98.31
	5	78.65

Based on the preceding table, you would eventually reach 100 percent depreciation. However, the table is prepared with the consideration in mind that you will have regular maintenance on the instrument. Without it, the depreciation rate will be much greater. But with care, proper maintenance, and good repairs, even after the 100 percent depreciation has been reached, your instrument will still not be without value.

It can have what Kenneth Neidig calls an "extra life." Mr. Neidig puts it this way:

> After the tenth year the director must estimate the remaining life expectancy. If he feels that another five years have been added by the repairs, then he will put aside one-fifth of the remaining net book valuation each year, adding the cost of any additional repairs to the net annual reserve for that year.[1]

In other words, even though an instrument may be said to have little, if any, resale value, it still will be worth something if you can still use it. But you should plan on replacing it with a comparably new instrument as soon as possible. It is startling how soon your whole department will consist of old instruments that will require a huge influx of funds to replace. If you wait until then to start replacing them, you will find it quite difficult to keep ahead of the depreciation.

Plan on a yearly purchase program to keep ahead of your depreciation rate, even if it means the acquisition of only one cornet or flute per year. That is better than trying to find the funds to purchase eight clarinets at once.

PROJECTING BUDGETS FOR PRICE INCREASES

Because of inflation and other price rises, the estimates for costs of items requisitioned in May or June may be different in August or September. The difference is usually going to be an *increase* in price. How can you account for this? One way is to set up a projected price increase of 10 percent for all items and budget organization. For example, if you have $1,000 to spend, you will set aside $100 for price increases. You actually now have a purchasing power of $900. This is a much better way than constantly going over your budget.

Should prices not increase, which is a rare phenomenon indeed, you will have a pleasant surprise and an extra $100 to spend on music supplies. But the 10 percent increase projection is important. It keeps your cost overruns down and keeps you within your budget. This establishes good relations with your business departments.

DOING PREVENTIVE MAINTENANCE ON PIANOS

Most music teachers are basically concerned with one aspect of a piano; keeping it tuned! That, however, is only part of the story. In order to maintain a piano properly and prevent undue depreciation (with care, a piano actually depreciates very little), you must have a program of proper maintenance. You must be concerned with such items as the sounding board, the condition of the strings, the pegs, all the mechanisms connected with the ivories (cleaning the insides of the keys), the exterior finish, wear and tear on the hinges, and other details.

Since most choral, band, orchestra, or general music teachers are not too familiar with piano mechanisms, you should avail yourself of the regular advice and services of a piano *technician*. Notice, we are not talking about a piano *tuner* only, but a piano technician. Many piano tuners advertise as such and do a most adequate job at tuning, but know very little about maintenance and repair.

Before you hire the services of a piano technician, seek his or her advice on the needed repairs or maintenance of your pianos. And make sure he or she is capable and willing to carry out all your maintenance needs. In other words, seek the advice of an expert—and use his or her expertise to make sure all pianos are in good playing condition.

THE IMPORTANCE OF STORING EQUIPMENT PROPERLY

Deterioration of equipment is inevitable, yet it can be slowed by the proper storing of instruments in temperature-controlled and fairly dry cabinets. Locks on cabinets will prevent temptation on the part of some students to handle unauthorized equipment.

If you have movable shelves on the instrument walls, you may wish to secure them and have doors built over them that can be secured with combination locks. Students who share the lockers will be given the combinations. The initial expense of constructing these lockers should become a saving in the long run by increased longevity of instruments and equipment.

ECONOMICAL WAYS TO MAKE YOUR ROOM ATTRACTIVE

Making your room attractive and efficient does not necessarily entail the requisitioning of expensive furniture and items of decoration. One way to make a room more attractive is to establish a student workday. Students are asked to bring in items they may have at home, such as paint, polish, photographs, plants, tables and chairs, and any other items that you feel would add to the beauty of the room.

Bookcases can be put up with the use of metal fixtures and cut boards, which are then varnished or painted according to your tastes. I once went to a secondhand store and bought a fine office desk and chair for $40, which then replaced the small wooden desk in the music office. That was five years ago, and the desk is still in use. A new one of the same type would have cost $350.

Once you have an idea of how the room should be set up, ask students to help in the redecoration of their room. They will usually respond enthusiastically to this challenge. The workday should be organized and carefully supervised, or the results from some of your less-skilled "helpers" may be less than satisfactory.

You can also ask for a parent workday or worknight. Many parents would be willing to help in the project if they were asked early enough and requested to do specific jobs. Adults usually do not have much spare time; therefore, do not let them waste time when they come. Be organized. Schedule painting and finishing touches after the carpentry or building is done.

It is really amazing just what can be accomplished with do-it-yourself decorations. Many teachers, however, take a defeatist attitude when it comes to no money in the budget for furnishings. It doesn't have to be that way. Give do-it-yourself decorations a try—you can really do wonders!

CHAPTER 12 ENDNOTES

1. Neidig, Kenneth L. *Music Director's Complete Handbook of Forms.* West Nyack, NY: Parker Publishing Co., 1973, 73.

Chapter 13

Teaching Tips for Wind Instruments

While there are books published on the band instruments, there is not a lot of help available for a quick reference on each instrument—including the points important for teaching, repertoire, solo lists, and specific idiosyncracies. This chapter solves that problem. Rather than an in-depth pedagogical treatment of each instrument, there are handy quick teaching tips, lists of works, method books, and solo material for each instrument.

TEACHING THE CLARINET

Certain difficulties in teaching young and advanced students on the clarinet can be overcome by observing some basic techniques. If these are adhered to, the instrument becomes far less difficult, and mastery is accelerated.

Teaching Techniques for Beginning Students

1. Embouchure
   a. Mouthpiece should be inserted only a small amount.
   b. Do not roll the lower lip; rather, cup it slightly.
   c. Rest upper teeth on the mouthpiece.
   d. Keep corners back slightly with jar open and "pointed" open.
2. Hand position
   a. Both hands are curved up slightly toward the mouthpiece.
   b. Fingers are down and close the keys.
   c. Right thumb resting so that thumbnail line is approximately in the middle of thumb rest.
3. Playing over the break
   a. No visible movement should occur in embouchure when octave key is pushed.
   b. Do not close the reed for higher notes.
   c. Keep breath strongly supported.

4. Tonguing
   a. Tongue *releases* the air; it does not "attack" the note.
   b. Tongue touches the reed only slightly.
   c. Breath support needed to back up the tongue motion.

Teaching Techniques for Advanced Students

1. High register
   a. The notes above High C tend to need a "special" feeling that may be different from that for other tones.
   b. Once students understand this, they can usually begin to "feel" this embouchure.
2. Development of technique
   a. Practice scales and arpeggios in all keys, major and minor, and in various articulations.
   b. Practice intervals such as 4ths, 5ths, and 8vas both slurred and tongued.
3. Improved reading
   a. Practice something previously unseen each day, preferably at a level just above student's present level.
   b. Use *Scales and Chords* by Gaston Hamelin, published by Alphonse-Leduc, Paris.

Method Books for Beginning Students

Clarinet Student, published by Belwin-Mills

Breeze-Easy Method, Volumes I and II, by Anzalone, published by Warner Brothers

Elementary Method by Hovey, published by Rubank Inc.

Universal-Fundamental Method by Pease, published by Universal

Universal Follow-Up, published by Universal

Beginning Method for Clarinet, published by Remick

Method Books for Intermediate Students

Intermediate Method by Skornicka Miller, published by Rubank Inc.
Daily Exercises and Scales by Pares, published by Fischer
Belwin Clarinet Method Book III, published by Belwin-Mills

Method Books for Advanced Students

Advanced Method, Volumes I & II by Voxman/Gower, published by Rubank Inc.
Selected Studies by Voxman, published by Rubank Inc.

Selected Easy Solo Literature for School Use

"Andanta & Gavotte" by Harris, published by Belwin-Mills
"Aria & Minuetto" by Mozart/Ayers, published by Barnhouse
"La Petite Rien" by Couperin/Honey, published by Rubank Inc.
"Lullaby" by Lagenus, published by Carl Fischer
"Serenade" by Buchtel, published by Kjos
"Theme & Variations" by Haydn/Kaplan, published by Jack Spratt

Selected Medium Solo Literature for School Use

"Concerto in G" by Handel, published by Andraud
"Giga" by Vivaldi/De Caprio, published by Warner Brothers
"Pastorale" by Reed, published by Edward Marks
"Romance" by Duport, published by Jack Spratt
"Scherzo" by Dittersdorf/Hanson, published by Ludwig
"Summer Nocturne" by Conley, published by Kendor
"Waltz" by Tchaikovsky/Harris, published by Ludwig

Selected Difficult Solo Literature for School Use

"Andante & Scherzo" by Dere/Hite, published by Southern Music Co.

"Concertino" by Weber, published by Carl Fischer

"Concertino" by White, published by Ludwig

"Prelude and Dance" by Richens, published by Kendor

"Rhapsodie" by Baeyens, published by Henri Elkan

"Sonatas No. 1 and No. 2" by Brahms, published by Carl Fischer

"Sonata for Clarinet and Piano" by Poulenc, published by J & W Chester

TEACHING THE FLUTE

Many students and some teachers take a simplistic view of the flute, and difficulties often occur because improper attention is paid to certain embouchure idiosyncrasies as well as the importance of good hand positions. The flute is *not* complicated, but is an instrument that requires sensitivity towards the aforementioned details. Success in later stages of playing is often based upon establishing solid fundamentals at the beginning.

Teaching Techniques for Beginning Students

1. Embouchure
   a. The embouchure is *not* like blowing across the top of soda bottles.
   b. Roll the flute outward as much as possible. Blow *into* and *across* the blow hole.
   c. High notes require the jaw thrust forward. Add a "pucker" or "oo" shape to the lips.
   d. Low notes require the jaw brought back. Stretch to an "ee" position for the lips.
2. Position
   a. Head is held up.
   b. Arms are away from the body.

   c. Fingers are curved *toward* the blow hole. Tips of fingers are held *just above* the keys.
   d. The tip of the finger is set across the entire key—not just the edge. Adjust angle of fingers accordingly.
3. Tonguing
   a. Tongue releases the air column.
   b. Articulate by the syllable "tah."
   c. Don't let student tongue between the teeth; make sure a solid "t" consonant is sounded, but *not* too hard.
   d. Practice with head joint alone.

Teaching Techniques for Advanced Students

1. High register
   a. Do not blow too much air across the hole without sufficiently covering the hole.
   b. Keep jaw forward, not just lips.
2. Development of technique
   a. Scales, keys, and arpeggios practiced in all registers, and keys with various articulations are the best technical development exercises you can do.
   b. Exercises for finger dexterity will include repetitive passages of difficult fingering patterns.
   c. Use "Grands Exercises Journaliers de Mecanisme pour Flute" by P. Taffanel and Ph. Gaubert, published by Alphonse-Leduc.
3. Improving reading
   a. Each day read through (without stopping) at least one new piece.
   b. Use *Melodious and Progressive Studies*, Books I, II, and III, by Robert Cavally, published by Southern Music Co.

Method Books for Beginning Students

Universal-Fundamental Method, published by Universal
Flute Student, published by Belwin-Mills

Elementary Method by Petersen, published by Rubank Inc.

Flute Method, Books I and II, published by Belwin-Mills

The Art and Practice of Modern Flute Techniques, published by MCA Music

Method Books for Intermediate Students

Intermediate Method by Skornicka/Petersen, published by Rubank Inc.

Melodious and Progressive Studies for Flute, Book I, published by Southern Music

24 Melodious Studies by Wummer, published by Carl Fischer

Method Books for Advanced Students

Advanced Method, Volumes I & II by Voxman/Gower, published by Rubank Inc.

Melodious and Progressive Studies, published by Southern Music

12 Studies by Boehm, published by Carl Fischer

Selected Easy Solo Literature for School Use

"Chanson Triste" by Burstahler, published by Pro Art

"Evening Reverie" by Frank, published by Kendor

"Piper" by Burstahler, published by Pro Art

"Reverie" by Guenther, published by Belwin-Mills

"Tango" by Buchtel, published by Kjos

"Tarantelle" by Buchtel, published by Kjos

"Valse Petite" by Hinkson, published by Rubank Inc.

Selected Medium Solo Literature for School Use

"Air" by Aubert/Barrere, published by G. Schirmer

"Andalouse" by Pessard, published by Alphonse-Leduc

"Calypso Song" by Feldsher, published by Aulos
"Mennett" by Kuhlan, published by Cundy-Bettony
"Petite Etude" by Dillon, published by Boosey & Hawkes
"Prelude" by Bergman, published by Schott
"Sonata in F Major" by Handel, published by Southern Music

Selected Difficult Solo Literature for School Use

"Concerto in D Major" by Mozart, published by Carl Fischer
"Gigue" by Hue, published by Oxford
"Petite Suite" by Pierre/Petit, published by Alphonse-Leduc
"Poem" by Doran, published by Western International Music
"Prelude et Air" by Denisov, published by Alphonse-Leduc
"Prelude and Rondo" by Tardos, published by Boosey & Hawkes
"Sonata" by Lane, published by Carl Fischer

TEACHING THE SAXOPHONE

While the saxophone is a relatively easy instrument for students to begin to play, this should not detract from the artistry required to play it well. Too often, however, this is neglected by teachers. The instrument is often equated with the clarinet. There are similarities, but there are also noticeable differences.

Teaching Techniques for Beginning Students

1. Embouchure
    a. More of the mouthpiece is put into the mouth than on a clarinet.
    b. The lower lip must not be rolled back too far.
    c. Keep the jaw open as far as possible. Point the chin.
2. Hand position
    a. The normal hand position is relatively easy to make. The fingers should only curve very slightly upward or remain perpendicular to the horn.

3. Playing through the octave
   a. The main difficulty imposed when playing through the octave is that the use of the octave key tends to make the upper note sharp. Students must be taught to listen extremely well so that the notes will sound "in tune." In short, do not use more pressure for the high notes, and use good breath support and listen.
4. Tonguing
   a. Do not "attack" the reed to articulate; rather, release the air stream. Precede each articulation with good breath support.

Teaching Techniques for Advanced Students

1. High register
   a. Relax the embouchure but use plenty of breath support.
   b. Keep the throat open at all times.
2. Development of technique
   a. Practice scales and arpeggios in all keys, major and minor, and in various articulations.
   b. Move the fingers *exactly* with the tongue.
   c. Keep the fingers not in use in position just over the keys.

Method Books for Beginning Students

Elementary Method by Hovey, published by Rubank Inc.

Breeze-Easy Method, Volumes I and II, by Anzalone, published by Warner Brothers

Saxophone Student, published by Belwin-Mills

Universal-Fundamental Method, published by Universal

Method Books for Intermediate Students

Intermediate Method by Skornicka, published by Rubank Inc.

Universal Follow-up Method, published by Universal

Belwin Method Book II, published by Belwin-Mills

Method Books for Advanced Students

Advanced Method, Volumes I & II, by Voxman/Gower, published by Rubank Inc.

Basic Technique by Snavely, published by Kendor

33 Concert Etudes, published by Carl Fischer

Selected Studies for Saxophone, Book 3, by Labanchi, published by Rubank Inc.

Selected Easy Solo Literature for School Use

"A Quempas Tune" by Rascher, published by Belwin-Mills

"Bouree" by Bach, published by Alphonse-Leduc

"Heather on the Hill" by Maltby, published by Kendor

"Hunters Chorus" by Weber/ Tascher, published by Belwin-Mills

"Minuet" by Fox/Rascher, published by Belwin-Mills

"Rondino" by Kreisler/Leeson, published by Charles Foley

Selected Medium Solo Literature for School Use

"Beyond These Hills" by Wirth, published by Studio PR

"Cantilena" by Benson, published by Boosey & Hawkes

"Oxen Minuet" by Haydn/Rascher, published by Belwin-Mills

"Sicilienne" by Lantier, published by Alphonse-Leduc

"Sonata, Op. 1, No. 7" by Vivaldi/Hunt, published by Carl Fischer

"Two Bourees" by Purcell/Rascher, published by Bourne

"Waltz for Juliet" by Fote, published by Kendor

Selected Difficult Solo Literature for School Use

"Aria by Bozza, published by Alphonse-Leduc

"Concerto" by Glazounov, published by Southern Music

"Episode" by Walters, published by Southern Music

"L'Abeille" by Schubert/Leeson, published by M. Baron Co.
"Sarabande & Gigue" by Tull, published by Boosey & Hawkes
"Sonata" by Telemann/Londeix, published by Alphonse-Leduc
"Sonata No. 5" by Platti/Hervig, published by Rubank Inc.

TEACHING THE OBOE

The oboe has been viewed as a very difficult instrument. Much care does need to be taken in playing and caring for the horn, yet with reasonable attention to the idiosyncrasies of the instrument, the oboe can be approached with confidence, and mastery can be attained.

Teaching Techniques for Beginning Students

1. Embouchure
   a. The upper lip is *not* rolled over the upper teeth while the lower lip *is* rolled over the lower teeth. Corners of the mouth are pulled in. Make sure there is equal pressure all around the reed. Keep the jaw open and keep a flat chin.
2. Hand position
   a. Lightly touch the keys with the fingertips and curve the fingers upwards slightly.
3. Tonguing
   a. The tip of the tongue touches just under the tip of the reed.

Teaching Techniques for Advanced Students

1. Half-hole techniques
   a. Let the first finger of the left hand cover the plate, but not the hole.
2. Vibrato
   a. The best method is considered to be diaphragm vibrato.
3. Double and triple tonguing
   a. Alternation between "t" and "k" syllables is the preferred method. However, as the speed increases, the

articulation should gradually become "d" and "g," a more relaxed tongue. This technique is not required often on the oboe.

4. Transposing English horn parts
   a. When playing English horn parts on the oboe, if possible, transpose down a fifth to sound the actual pitch. Since some notes will be too low, transpose up a fourth.

Method Books for Beginning Students

Breeze-Easy Method, Volumes I and II, by Anzalone, published by Warner Brothers

Oboe Student, published by Belwin-Mills

Gekeler Method, Volumes I and II, by Gekeler, published by Belwin-Mills

Method Books for Intermediate Students

Intermediate Method by Skornicka, published by Rubank Inc.

Gekeler Method, Volume III, by Gekeler, published by Belwin-Mills

A Method for Oboe, published by University Music Press

Method Books for Advanced Students

Advanced Method, Volumes I & II, by Voxman/Gower, published by Rubank Inc.

Complete Method by Barret, published by Boosey & Hawkes

Selected Studies by Voxman, published by Rubank Inc.

Basic Techniques for Oboe, published by Kendor

Selected Easy Solo Literature for School Use

"Anitra's Dance" by Grieg/Tustin, published by Barnhouse

"Barcarolle" by Labate, published by Carl Fischer

"Humming Song" by Schumann, published by Belwin-Mills

"Meditation" by Buchtel, published by Kjos
"Pastorale" by Butterworth, published by Boosey & Hawkes
"Pastorale" by Bakaleinikov, published by Belwin-Mills
"Polka" by Erickson, published by Belwin-Mills

Selected Medium Solo Literature for School Use

"Andantino" by Tchaikovsky, published by Carl Fischer
"Arioso" by Bach, published by Carl Fischer
"Bagatelle" by Beethoven/Hanson, published by Ludwig
"Sinfonia" by Bach, published by Carl Fischer
"Slavonic Dance" by Dvorak, published by Carl Fischer
"Two Themes by Handel" by Krenek, published by Belwin-Mills
"Vocalise" by Rachmaninov, published by Edition-Musicus

Selected Difficult Solo Literature for School Use

"Concertino" by Jakma, published by Henri Elkan
"Concertino in G Minor" by Handel, published by Rubank Inc.
"Concerto in F Minor" by Telemann, published by Andraud
"First Concertino" by Gilhaud, published by Rubank Inc.
"Pastorale" by Hanson, published by Carl Fischer
"Sonata No. 3" by Handel, published by Andraud
"Sonata No. 6 in G Minor" by Vivaldi/Marx, published by McGinnis & Marx

TEACHING THE BASSOON

A rather easy instrument to produce sounds on, the bassoon requires special attention to the embouchure in order to develop the full, rich, and resonant tone expected. With proper attention to this detail, the instrument is very satisfying for young students to play. Progress should be smooth and steady.

Teaching Techniques for Beginning Students

1. Embouchure
   a. Both lips should cover the teeth with the upper lip close to the wire of the reed.
   b. Keep chin back a little with the lower lip near the tip of the reed.
   c. Do not bunch up the chin; point it.
2. Hand position
   a. Make sure the hand rest is lined up in the right position so that the seat strap and hand rest (if used) coordinate the hand and general posture positions.
3. Tonguing
   a. Touch the tip of the blades of the reed. The articulation is actually a *release* rather than an attack.
   b. Stop the tone with the air and silently replace tongue on reed.

Teaching Techniques for Advanced Students

1. Staccato tonguing
   a. Do not articulate the end of the note "taht" or "tut." Instead, keep it open "ta" or "tu." This will insure resonance in the note to be heard and prevent a "pecking" sound.
   b. Do not make the staccato too short or the pecking sound will occur.
   c. Do not make any facial movements while tonguing.
2. Intonation
   a. Exert more pressure on the reed and raise the back of the tongue higher in order to raise the pitch.
   b. Use less pressure and lower the back of the tongue to lower the pitch.
3. Technique
   a. Keep finger movement to a minimum. Keep fingers close to keys.

b. Practice 16th notes at various metronome markings to improve the technique.

4. High register
   a. Use more reed for the high notes and also increase breath support and intensity.

Method Books for Beginning Students

Breeze-Easy Method, Volumes I and II, by Anzalone, published by Warner Brothers

Bassoon Method, Volumes I and II, published by Belwin-Mills

Elementary Method by Skornicka, published by Rubank Inc.

Method Books for Intermediate Students

Intermediate Method by Voxman, published by Rubank Inc.

Bassoon Method, Volume II, published by Belwin-Mills

Method Books for Advanced Students

Advanced Method, Volume I, by Voxman/Gower, published by Rubank Inc.

20 Studies for Bassoon by Vaulet/Voxman, published by Rubank Inc.

Selected Easy Solo Literature for School Use

"Alma Del Core" by Caldara/Cacavas, published by Belwin-Mills

"Air" by Penn, published by Lake State Publications

"Brook" by Organn, published by Rebo Music Co.

"Cantilena" by Handel/Buchtel, published by Kjos

"Minuet in G Major" by Bach, published by Medici Music Co.

"Romance Melody" by Glinka/Schumann, published by Jack Spratt

"Waltz for Juliet" by Fote, published by Kendor

Selected Medium Solo Literature for School Use

"Adelaide" by Beethoven, published by Kendor
" Clair de Lune " by Debussy, published by Edition Musicus
"Air Rhythm & Legend" by Allard, published by Theodore Presser
"Contrasts" by Siegmeister, published by MCA Music
"For He That Is Mighty" by Bach, published by Kendor
"Romanze" by Klughardt, published by Carl Fischer
"Sarabande" by Debussy/Paine, published by Belwin-Mills

Selected Difficult Solo Literature for School Use

"Burlesque" by Bozza, published by Alphonse-Leduc
"Ciranda Das Notas" by Villa-Lobos, published by Peer Southern Organization
"Concerto No. 2 in B Flat" by Mozart, published by Henry Litolff's Verlag
"Introduction & Scherzo" by Wagner, published by Southern Music
"Solo De Concert" by Pierne, published by Carl Fischer
"Three Pieces" by Stevens, published by C. F. Peters
"Trois Nocturnes" by Duclos, published by Alphonse-Leduc

TEACHING THE TRUMPET AND CORNET

The trumpet and cornet are two of the instruments that present the least amount of difficulty for beginning students. Progress is normally fairly rapid and steady. As a result, however, there sometimes is a tendency to overlook some bad habits and problems as they occur. Below are some aids to prevent problems and correct those that appear.

Teaching Techniques for Beginning Students

1. Embouchure
   a. While the basic embouchure is one-third upper and two-thirds lower, there are so many variations that this cannot readily be insisted upon.
   b. Students should concentrate on the aperture once the basic embouchure is formed.
   c. The aperture should be basically shaped like a football. Concentrating on this will keep the tone open, free, and resonant.
2. Hand position
   a. Keep the left hand relaxed when gripping the instrument.
   b. The right-hand fingers should be rounded with the tips touching the keys. Keep the little finger out of the ring brace.
3. Tonguing
   a. Use "ta" or "tu" syllables, but do not end the tone with the tongue, as in "tut." This interferes both with the resonance and with the breath support.

Teaching Techniques for Advanced Students

1. Double and triple tonguing
   a. As the tonguing goes faster, the syllable "ta-ka" or "ta-ta-ka" should gradually change to a "d" or "g" sound as in "da-ga" or "da-da-ga." This relaxes the tongue, allowing an increase in speed without constricting or tiring the muscles.
2. Vibrato
   a. The most common form of vibrato used by professionals is the hand vibrato.
   b. Slightly shaking the right hand will produce this type.
   c. Some players use diaphragm vibrato, which can be effective if controlled properly.

Method Books for Beginning Students

Breeze Easy Methods, Volumes I and II, by Anzalone, published by Warner Brothers

Elementary Method by Robinson, published by Rubank Inc.

Universal Method, published by Universal

Method Books for Intermediate Students

Intermediate Method by Skornicka, published by Rubank Inc.

Arban Method (abridged) by Arban, published by Carl Fischer

Supplementary Method by Endresen, published by Rubank Inc.

Method Books for Advanced Students

Advanced Methods, Volumes I & II, by Voxman/Gower, published by Rubank Inc.

Characteristic Studies by Clarke, published by Carl Fischer

Selected Studies, published by Rubank Inc.

Arban Method (complete) by Arban, published by Carl Fischer

Selected Easy Solo Literature for School Use

"Bolero" by Buchtel, published by Kjos

"Conversation for Cornet" by Grundman, published by Boosey & Hawkes

"Londonderry Air" by Buchtel, published by Kjos

"Lazy Day" by Myers, published by Lake State Publications

"March of the Matadores" by Eymann, published by Pro Art

"Minuetto" by Beethoven/Stouffer, published by Kindor

"To a Wild Rose" by MacDowell/Isaac, published by Carl Fischer

Selected Medium Solo Literature for School Use

"Achilles" by Endresen, published by Rubank Inc.
"Air & Dance" by Corelli, published by Edition Musicus
"Ave Marie" by Bruckner, published by Edition Musicus
"Call" by Fitzgerald, published by Carl Fischer
"Legend" by Bakaleinikov, published by Belwin-Mills
"Reverie" by Glantz, published by Charles Colin
"Sonata in F Major" by Benda, published by Belwin-Mills

Selected Difficult Solo Literature for School Use

"Concertino" by Porrino, published by G. Ricordi
"Concertino" by Vidal, published by Belwin-Mills
"First Concert Piece" by Brandt, published by Cundy-Bettony
"Rondo Capriccio" by Fitzgerald, published by Carl Fischer
"Sonata No. 1" by Abel/Kinney, published by Studio PR
"Sonatino" by White, published by Shawnee Press
"Valse Caprice" by Liberati, published by Ludwig

TEACHING THE TROMBONE AND BARITONE

It has been said that of all the instruments, the trombone most closely resembles the human voice in its manner of playing. Because of the use of a slide, rather than valves or keys, the instrument is capable of nearly perfect intonation. Breath support, openness of the throat, and the use of one's ear contribute to this relationship. As a result, the instrument is both versatile in expression and consistent in natural tone quality. A few problems can be avoided if strategic aspects of the instrument are concentrated on.

Teaching Techniques for Beginning Students

1. Embouchure
    a. One might consider that three-quarters of the mouthpiece is above the center line of the lips, with one-quarter

below. (A relationship that feels closer to two-thirds upper, one-third lower may also be used.)

b. Keep the jaw as open as possible.

2. Arm-hand position
   a. Two fingers on top and two below are the standard grip for the slide arm. The right arm must, however, remain relaxed.
3. Tonguing
   a. Use the syllable "tu" for a rich, full tone. Never say "tut" unless a specific effect is needed.
4. Breathing
   a. The breath support should always be diaphragmatic, exactly as in vocal music.

Teaching Techniques for Advanced Students

1. Double and triple tonguing
   a. As with the trumpet and cornet, the faster you go in double or triple tonguing, the more you will change from a "tu-ku" or "tu-tu-ku" tongue to a "du-gu" or "du-du-gu" one. This relaxes the tongue and allows it to speed up easily.
2. Vibrato
   a. The jaw or embouchure vibrato and the slide vibrato are the two recommended methods for the trombone. The slide vibrato is used mainly for swing or dance bands while the jaw vibrato is used in the symphonic form. Both can be interchangeable if done with taste.

Method Books for Beginning Students

Trombone Student, published by Belwin-Mills

Universal-Fundamental Method, published by Universal

Breeze Easy Methods, Volumes I and II, by Anzalone, published by Warner Brothers

Elementary Method by Long, published by Rubank Inc.

Method Books for Intermediate Students

Intermediate Method by Skornicka/Boltz, published by Rubank Inc.

Etudes for Trombone by Vandercook, published by Rubank Inc.

Supplementary Studies by Endresen, published by Rubank Inc.

Method Books for Advanced Students

Advanced Methods, Volumes I & II, Voxman/Gower, published by Rubank Inc.

Selected Studies by Voxman, published by Rubank Inc.

Famous Method of Slide and Valve Trombone and Baritone by Arban Crandall Mantia, published by Carl Fischer

Selected Easy Solo Literature for School Use

"Andantino Cantable" by Bakaleinikov, published by Belwin-Mills

"Aurora" by Faure/Stoutamire, published by Kendor

"Berceuse" by Concone/Gower, published by Rubank Inc.

"My Heart at Thy Sweet Voice" by Saint-Saens/Goldman, published by Carl Fischer

"Powdered Wig" by McKay, published by Barnhouse

"Romance" by Rubinstein/Smith, published by Belwin-Mills

"To a Wild Rose" by MacDowell, published by Alphonse-Leduc

Selected Medium Solo Literature for School Use

"Clair de Lune" by Debussy, published by Edition Musicus

"Arioso" by Cirri/Forst, published by Edition Musicus

"Contest Piece" by Alary, published by Cundy-Bettony

"Cortege" by Whitney, published by Bourne

"Elegy" by Martin, published by Carl Fischer

"For He That Is Mighty" by Bach/Figert, published by Kendor

"Northern Dance" by Hill, published by Gordon V. Thompson

Selected Difficult Solo Literature for School Use

"Cortege" by Dubois, published by Alphonse-Leduc
"Curves of Gold" by Coolidge, published by Kendor
"Estrella" by Smith, published by Carl Fischer
"Meditation" by Jacobi, published by Peer-Southern Organization
"Rondo" by Beethoven, published by Edition Musicus
"Sonata" by Bassett, published by King
"Sonata" by Kelly, published by Tritone

TEACHING THE FRENCH HORN

There are several misconceptions regarding the French horn. These need to be clarified in order to alleviate some confusion. The horn, although difficult to play, is not as difficult to teach as has been popularly thought. The suggestions given below should be of great aid in helping students master this very melodious and beautiful instrument.

Teaching Techniques for Beginning Students

1. Embouchure
   a. The horn embouchure differs from the trumpet or cornet in this way: two-thirds of upper lip and one-third lower lip should be in the mouthpiece, as opposed to the more generally accepted 50/50 proportion on the trumpet.
   b. The upper (inserted portion) lip is pushed slightly forward with the corners of the embouchure only slightly pulled back. This minor difference plays a very important role in tonal development.
2. Right hand position
   a. The right hand should be thought of as an extension of the bell itself.
   b. Do not leave any open holes between the fingers.
   c. Keep the fingers straight.

   d. Cup the palm at about a 45 degree angle and lay the back of the hand on the bottom of the bell.

3. Tonguing
   a. Use the syllable "tu" always. Never say "ta." This helps in keeping the embouchure correctly formed and the tone rich and mellow.
4. Breathing
   a. Diaphragmatic breathing should be the *only* kind used. Never allow the student to breath in any other manner since it will interfere with developing a full, rich, and sonorous tone.

Teaching Technique for Advanced Students

1. Low register
   a. The low register needs to be broken in on the horn. This can be accomplished by arpeggios slurred and repeated note patterns increasing in volume to as loud as possible.
2. High register
   a. The high register should be increased one note at a time only after meeting the following conditions: Low register is developing correctly; there is no change in embouchure to reach the high notes; and the aperture (actual opening in the embouchure through which the air flows) is as open as possible.

Method Books for Beginning Students

Elementary Method by Skornicka, published by Rubank Inc.

Universal-Fundamental Method, published by Universal

Breeze Easy Method, Volumes I and II, by Anzalone, published by Warner Brothers

Method Books for Intermediate Students

Intermediate Method by Skornicka/Erdman, published by Rubank Inc.

Alphonse-Leduc Method, Books I and II, published by Alphonse-Leduc

Method Books for Advanced Students

Advanced Method, Volumes I & II, by Voxman/Gower, published by Rubank Inc.

335 Selected Melodious & Progressive Studies by Pottag/Andraud, published by Southern Music Co.

Selected Easy Solo Literature for School Use

"Autumn Dream" by Lotzenhiser, published by Belwin-Mills.
"Hunters" by Hill, published by Kjos
"Impressions" by Ward, published by Kendor
"Lazy Day" by Myers, published by Lake State Publications
"Meadowland" by Hurrell, published by Rubank Inc.
"Romance" by Scriabin, published by Leeds
"Serenade" by Kaplan, published by Belwin-Mills

Selected Medium Solo Literature for School Use

"Ballad for Horn" by Butts, published by Barnhouse
"Cabaletta" by Klauss, published by Pro Art
"Chant Corse" by Tomasi, published by Alphonse-Leduc
"Little Rondo" by Beethoven, published by G. Schirmer
"Lullaby" by Cox, published by Jack Spratt
"Moods for Horn" by Atkinson, published by Schmitt, Hall and McCreary Co.
"Nocturne" by Anderson, published by Carl Fischer

Selected Difficult Solo Literature for School Use

"Adagio and Allegro" by Haddad, published by Shawnee Press
"Aria" by Hamilton, published by Schott

"Aubade" by Gagnebin, published by Alphonse-Leduc
"Concert Piece" by Sibbing, published by Tenuto
"Elegia" by Satatini, published by Cor Publishing
"En Irlande" by Bozza, published by Alphonse-Leduc
"Morceau de Concert" by Saint-Saens, published by International Music Co.

TEACHING THE TUBA

One of the biggest misconceptions about the tuba is that it is often considered only as a harmony instrument, generally sticking to the root of the chord or its inversions. A second error is in the thinking that it supplies mainly the rhythmic impetus too often associated with the "oom-pah-pah" stereotypes. While these ideas have their place, the instrument has become a melody instrument of solo caliber in its own right. The instrumentalist must approach the tuba with the same sense of potential musicality as any of the "traditional" melody instruments; when it is viewed in this light, the teacher and student will arrive at a greater appreciation of the velvet-rich tonal possibilities of this very versatile horn.

Teaching Techniques for Beginning Students

1. Embouchure
    a. There seems to be more latitude as to the exact spot for tuba mouthpiece placement. Nevertheless, the student should strive to find the ideal spot. This is done mainly by feel.
2. Tone quality
    a. The embouchure should be firm within the corners of the mouth.
    b. The cheeks should not puff out and the jaw should be down and relaxed. Any error in this will adversely affect tone color.
3. Tonguing
    a. Facial and jaw movement should be avoided at all times.

b. Use the tongue only in attacking tones and use a "tu" syllable.

4. Breathing

a. Unless a constant flow of air is used, and a big diaphragmatic breath is taken in, the tone will not be sustained nor will it have the same quality in all registers.

Teaching Techniques for Advanced Students

1. Double and triple tonguing

a. As with the trombone, the faster the tempo, the more relaxed the tongue must be. Go from a "tu-ku" to a "du-gu" sound.

2. Vibrato

a. The jaw vibrates to the recommended style for tuba solos.

Method Books for Beginning Students

Elementary Method by Hovey, published by Rubank Inc.

Universal-Fundamental Method, published by Universal

Breeze Easy Method, Volumes I and II, by Anzalone, published by Warner Brothers

Method Books for Intermediate Students

Intermediate Method by Skornicka/Boltz, published by Rubank Inc.

The Geib Method by Geib, published by Carl Fischer

60 Musical Studies for Tuba, Book II, published by Southern Music Co.

Method Books for Advanced Students

Advanced Methods, Volumes I and II, by Voxman/Gower, published by Rubank Inc.

70 Studies by Blazhevich, published by Robert King

Selected Easy Solo Literature for School Use

"Bouree" by Handel/Swanson, published by Belwin-Mills
"Blow the Man Down" by Walters, published by Rubank Inc.
"Deep River" by Harris, published by Cundy-Bettony
"Gavotte" by Bell, published by Carl Fischer
"Russian Melody" by Bell, published by Belwin-Mills
"Venetian Carnival" by Bowles, published by Belwin-Mills
"Wotan" by Buchtel, published by Kjos

Selected Medium Solo Literature for School Use

"Andanta" by Handel/Ostrander, published by Edition Musicus
"Ballad for Tuba" by Christensen, published by Kendor
"Carnival of Venice" by Holmes, published by Rubank Inc.
"Chansonnoir" by Burgstahler, published by Pro Art
"Deep Rock" by Bowles, published by Belwin-Mills
"Nautical John" by Bell, published by Carl Fischer
"Sonatina for Tuba" by Sear, published by Cor Publishing

Selected Difficult Solo Literature for School Use

"Concertino for Tuba" by Frackenpohl, published by King
"Emmett's Lullabye" by Holmes, published by Rubank Inc.
"Fantasy a Due" by Reed, published by Belwin-Mills
"Fantasy for Tuba" by Arnold, published by Faber
"Serenade" by Schmidt, published by Western International Music
"Sonata" by Hindemith, published by Schott
"Suite for Tuba" by Haddad, published by Shawnee Press

BIBLIOGRAPHY

Abdoo, Frank B. "A Recording System for Your Program." *Music Educators Journal* (March 1981): 59.

Adler, Marvin S., and Jesse C. McCarroll. *Elementary Teachers Music Almanac*. West Nyack, NY: Parker Publishing Co., 1978.

Alexander, Carolyn. "Organizing Beyond the Textbooks." *Music Educators Journal* (January 1981): 50.

Baker, Don R. "Percussion Maintenance and Repair." *The Instrumentalist* (February 1981): 62.

Brand, Manny. "The Challenge of the First Year" *Music Educators Journal* (September 1981): 35.

Brown, Frank. *A Band Director's Handbook of Problems and Solutions in Teaching Instrumental Music*. Lebanon, IN: Studio PR, 1979.

Combs, Michael F. "Timpani Repair and Maintenance," *Music Educators Journal (February 1980): 56.*

Cope, David. *New Directions in Music*. Dubuque, IA: William C. Brown, 1971.

Cope, David. *"The Mechanics of Listening to Electronic Music."* *Music Educators Journal* (October 1977): 47.

Dackow, Sandra. "A Proposal for Chamber Music in the High School Curriculum." *Music Educators Journal* (May 1981): 38.

Dynan, Robert J. "A Way Out of the Pep Band Predicament." *Music Educators Journal (May 1980): 44.*

Farkas, Philip. *The Art of Horn Playing*. Evanston, IL: Summy-Birchard, 1956.

Farkas, Philip. *The Art of Brass Playing*. Bloomington, IN: Brass Publications. 1962.

Farnsworth, Roger W. "Tape Tutelage." *Music Educators Journal* (April 1981): 40.

Glenn, Neal E., William B. McBride, and George Wilson. *Secondary School Music*. Englewood Cliffs, NJ: Prentice-Hall, 1970.

Grout, Donald J. *A History of Western Music*. New York: W. W. Norton & Company, 1973.

Hughes, James R., "How Do You Behave? Your Non-verbal Actions Are Critical to Student Motivation." *Music Educators Journal* (January 1981): 52.

Intravia, Lawrence, J. *Building a Superior School Band Library*. West Nyack, NY: Parker Publishing Co., 1972.

Jacobs, Ruth. "The Easy Numbers Game for Guitar." *Music Educators Journal* (April 1981): 42.

Jacques-Dalcroze, Emile. *Rhythm, Music and Education.* London: Dalcroze Society, 1921.

Jipson, Wayne R. *The High School Vocal Music Program.* West Nyack, NY: Parker Publishing Co., 1972.

Jones, Arnold. "Music Education and 'Back to the Basics.' " *The School Musician* (March 1981): 6.

Kinney, Guy. "Concert Programming: Tips from the Broadcast Industry." *Music Educators Journal* (December 1978): 44.

Kinney, Guy S. *Complete Guide to Teaching Small Instrumental Groups in the High School.* West Nyack, NY: Parker Publishing Co., 1980.

Kinney, Guy S. "Developing a Comprehensive High School Curriculum." *School Music News* (March 1980): 34.

Kleinhammer, Edward. *The Art of Trombone Playing.* Evanston, IL: Summy-Birchard, 1963.

Labuta, Joseph A. *Guide to Accountability in Music Instruction.* West Nyack, NY: Parker Publishing Co., 1974.

Larsen, Arved M. "An Overlooked Teaching Aid: Films Can Make the Difference." *Music Educators Journal* (December 1980): 32.

Luening, Otto. "History of Electronic Music." *Music Educators Journal* (November 1968): 42.

Mager, Robert F. *Preparing Instructional Objectives.* Palo Alto, CA: Fearon Publishers, 1962.

Michaels, Arthur J. "12 Ways to Get the Most Out of Your Budget." *Music Educators Journal* (January 1981): 40.

Mills, Donn Laurence. "If I Only Had Less Rehearsal Time." *The Instrumentalist* (January 1981): 82.

Moss, Orlando. *Complete Handbook for Teaching Small Vocal Ensembles.* West Nyack, NY: Parker Publishing Co., 1978.

Neidig, Kenneth L. *Music Director's Complete Handbook of Forms.* West Nyack, NY: Parker Publishing Co., 1973.

Neilson, James. "Accountability/Responsibility.' *The School Musician* (June/July 1980): 38.

Pence, Homer. *Teacher's Complete Guide to the Bassoon.* Elkhart, IN: Selmer Co., 1963.

Putnik, Edwin. *The Art of Flute Playing.* Evanston, IL: Summy-Birchard, 1973.

Schmitt, Sister Cecelia. "Personal Effectiveness with Your Students." *The Instrumentalist* (September 1978): 44.

Shetler, Donald J. "A Director's Guide to Public Relations and Promotions." *The Instrumentalist* (August 1976): 40.

Smith, Charles W. "Duplets, Triplets, and Quadruplets." *The Instrumentalist* (April 1981): 11.

Sperl, Gary. "Woodwind Instrument Maintenance." *Music Educators Journal* (March 1980): 46.

Sprenkle, Robert, and Robert Ledet. *The Art of Oboe Playing.* Evanston, IL: Summy-Birchard, 1961.

Stanley, Burton. "Instrument Repair for the Band Man" (one in a series of articles in *School Music News*, December 1970, November 1971, January 1972, February 1972, April 1972, and September 1975).

Stein, Keith. *The Art of Clarinet Playing.* Evanston, IL: Summy-Birchard, 1958.

Stuart, Jesse. *To Teach, to Love.* New York: World Publishing Co., 1970.

Tiede, Clayton H. *The Practical Band Instrument Repair Manual.* Dubuque, IA: William C. Brown Co., 1970.

Weerts, Richard. *Developing Individual Skills for the High School Band.* West Nyack, NY: Parker Publishing Co., 1969.

Weerts, Richard. *How to Develop and Maintain a Successful Woodwind Section.* West Nyack, NY: Parker Publishing Co., 1972.

Weerts, Richard. *Handbook of Rehearsal Techniques for the High School Band.* West Nyack, NY: Parker Publishing Co., 1976.

Westphal, Frederick. *Guide to Teaching Woodwinds.* Dubuque, IA: William C. Brown Co., 1981.

Young, Amanda. "Win the Funding Game." *Music Educators Journal* (November 1981) 43.

Index

O

P

R